The
French Bulldog

An Owner's Guide To

A HAPPY HEALTHY PET

Howell Book House

IDG Books Worldwide, Inc.
An International Data Group Company
Foster City, CA • Chicago, IL • Indianapolis, IN • New York, NY

Howell Book House
IDG Books Worldwide, Inc.
An International Data Group Company
919 E. Hillsdale Boulevard
Suite 400
Foster City, CA 94404

For general information on IDG Books Worldwide's books in the U.S., please
call our Consumer Customer Service department at 800-762-2974. For reseller
information, including discounts and premium sales, please call our Reseller
Customer Service department at 800-434-3422.

Library of Congress Cataloging-in-Publication Data
Dannel, Kathy.
       The French bulldog/[Kathy Dannel].
       p. cm.—(An Owner's guide to a happy healthy pet)
       Includes bibliographical references (p.)
       ISBN 1-58245-163-X
       1. French bulldog. I. Title. II. Series.
       SF429.F8 D36 2000
       636.72—dc21   00-035054

Manufactured in the United States of America
10 9 8 7 6 5 4 3 2 1

Series Director: Susanna Thomas
Book Design by Michele Laseau
Cover Design by Iris Jeromnimon
External Features Illustration by Shelley Norris
Other Illustrations by Jeff Yesh
Photography:
  Front and back cover by Mary Bloom
  All interioer photography by Mary Bloom except as indicated.
    Joan Balzarini: 96
    Paulette Braun/Pets by Paulette: 96
    Buckinghambill American Cocker Spaniels: 148
    Sian Cox: 134
    Dr. Ian Dunbar: 98, 101, 103, 111, 116–117, 122, 123, 127
    Dan Lyons: 96
    Cathy Merrithew: 129
    Liz Palika: 133
    Susan Rezy: 96–97
    Judith Strom: 96, 107, 110, 128, 130, 135, 137, 139, 140, 144, 149, 150
Production Team: Stephanie Lucas, Heather Pope, and Linda Quigley

Contents

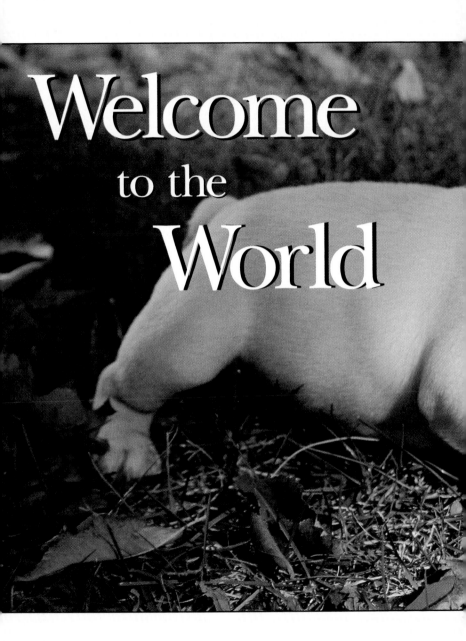

Welcome
to the
World

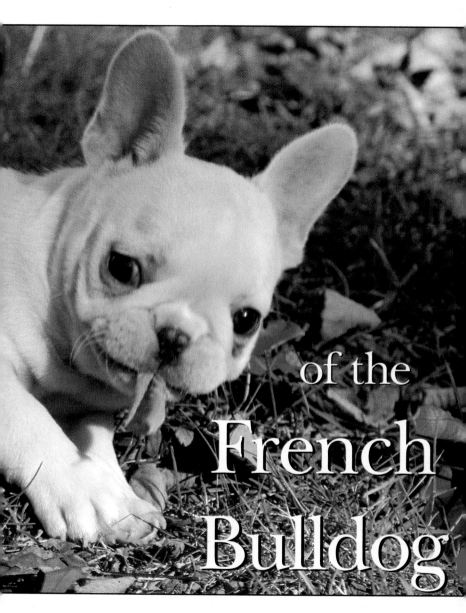

of the

French

Bulldog

External Features of the French Bulldog

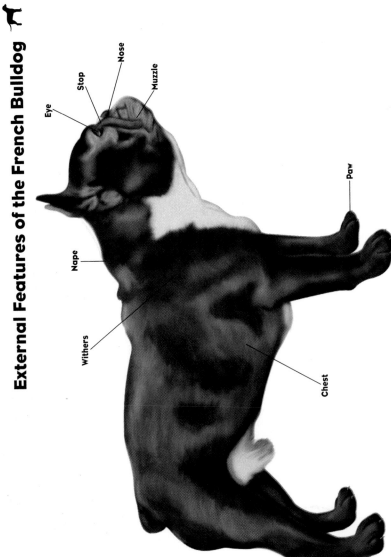

Eye

Stop

Nose

Muzzle

Nape

Withers

Paw

Chest

chapter 1

What Is a French Bulldog?

Imagine an enormous pair of bat ears and a flat, monkey-like face with shiny shoe-button eyes atop the sleek, muscular physique of a little canine bodybuilder. Roll all of this into the friendliest package possible, add a dash of stubbornness and now you have a French Bulldog, or a Frenchie as they are often called.

Frenchies come in a spectrum of colors. Their short coats guarantee them to be virtually wash and wear. Their small to medium size allows them to be the perfect apartment dog, yet many French Bulldogs enjoy the life of a country dog. The Frenchie's easygoing temperament makes him an excellent children's companion. (Just do not subject a Frenchie to unsupervised attention from toddlers.)

French Bulldogs also make wonderful companions for the elderly or disabled. They seem to intuitively know to scale their energy level to accommodate the person they are with. Many French Bulldogs are involved in therapy work.

If a dog that will jog for miles or be a crackerjack obedience star is what you are looking for, a French Bulldog is not for you. But if you want a charming little companion with a whimsical sense of humor, the Frenchie will suit you perfectly. All a Frenchie really needs is someone to love and to be his "special person."

WHAT IS A BREED STANDARD?

A Breed Standard—a detailed description of an individual breed—is meant to portray the ideal specimen of that breed. This includes ideal structure, temperament, gait, type—all aspects of the dog. Because the standard describes an ideal specimen, it isn't based on any particular dog. It is a concept against which judges compare actual dogs and breeders strive to produce dogs. At a dog show, the dog that wins is the one that comes closest, in the judges' opinion, to the standard for its breed. Breed standards are written by the breed parent clubs, the national organizations formed to oversee the well-being of the breed. They are voted on and approved by the members of the parent clubs.

Introduction to the Standard

Each and every breed of dog, as recognized by the American Kennel Club, is required to have a "standard" or outline of what the perfect dog of that breed should be. This standard is what responsible breeders aspire to in planning a breeding program. Each breeding should be done with the standard as a goal to work toward. There are no "perfect" dogs, but breeders must work toward the ideal and continue to improve the breed. Other countries and groups of countries also have standards for each breed. These standards often differ from the AKC standard but are generally remarkably similar. In French Bulldogs, the greatest variance seems to be in colors allowed and size requirements (or lack thereof).

The French Bulldog standard in the United States was originally written in 1911 and underwent a major review in 1925. It was modified again in 1947 and then again in 1991. Most of the modifications have centered around color.

Interpreting the Standard

It has been said that a standard has as many interpretations as people reading it! Words and descriptions that had one general meaning in the early 1900s may now have a slightly different connotation. It is up to breeders and judges to do their best to interpret the standard in a generally acceptable manner.

Why Do We Have a Standard?

There must be a yardstick by which to measure; otherwise, each person's measurements would vary widely. "Medium to small structure" to one person may mean 10 to 15 pounds, and to another it may mean 25 to 30 pounds. Therefore, a standard is necessary to keep us all on the same wavelength. Otherwise, French Bulldogs would have no consistency at all.

Reputable breeders use the standard as a goal and breed to achieve that goal. It is incredibly difficult to breed dogs that always fit the standard, but this is what good breeders must do to continue to improve each breed. Often it is a very minor point that keeps a dog from meeting the standard and determines the difference between pet and show quality.

Dog shows are where breeders compete with each other to see how each dog measures up to the standard. Each day at a dog show, different AKC-approved judges compare each entry to the standard and select the best one, in their opinion, on that day in each category. As you might imagine, this can be a very interesting procedure.

Even if your dog doesn't measure up to the standard, he will still be a wonderful pet!

The French Bulldog Standard

You may obtain a complete copy of the French Bulldog standard from the American Kennel Club,

7

5580 Centerview Dr., Suite 200, Raleigh, NC 27606-3390. You also can call 212-696-8200 or visit www.akc.org. You may also contact the French Bulldog Club of America by calling 205-553-3817 or visiting www.frenchbulldog.org/fbdca.

Excerpts from the standard are below in italics, with the author's comments following. This standard was approved June 10, 1991, and became effective July 31, 1991.

THE AMERICAN KENNEL CLUB

Commonly referred to as the AKC, the American Kennel Club is a nonprofit organization devoted to the advancement of purebred dogs. The AKC maintains a registry of recognized breeds and adopts and enforces rules for dog events including shows, obedience trials, field trials, hunting tests, lure coursing, herding, earthdog trials, agility and the Canine Good Citizen program. It is a club of clubs established in 1884 and composed, today, of more than 500 autonomous dog clubs throughout the United States. Each club is represented by a delegate; the delegates make up the legislative body of the AKC, voting on rules and electing directors. The AKC maintains the Stud Book—a record of every dog ever registered with the AKC—and publishes a variety of materials on purebred dogs including a monthly magazine, books and numerous educational pamphlets. For more information, contact the AKC at the address listed in the "Resources" chapter, and look for the names of its publications in the chapter on "Recommended Reading."

OFFICIAL STANDARD FOR THE FRENCH BULLDOG

General Appearance

The French Bulldog has the appearance of an active, intelligent, muscular dog of heavy bone, smooth coat, compactly built and of medium to small structure. Expression alert, curious and interested. Any other alteration other than removal of dewclaws is considered a mutilation and is a disqualification.

Frenchies should look like a lot of dog in a medium to small package. They have a very dense mass in relation to their size (which is one reason they do not swim well). "Heavy bone" means the bone should seem substantial, never refined. A French Bulldog should never be mistaken for a Boston Terrier. Tails are never docked, and ears are never cropped—*never*.

Proportion and Symmetry

All points are well distributed and bear good relation one to the other; No feature being in such prominence from either excess or lack of quality that the animal appears poorly proportioned.

"Balance" is the word that comes to mind. The overall impression should be a solid, compact dog. The head should not be hugely out of proportion, even though the Frenchie is often referred to as a "head" breed. The legs should not be too long, and no one part should immediately catch your eye when you look at a Frenchie.

Size, Proportion, Substance
Weight not to exceed 28 pounds; over 28 pounds is a disqualification.

This is very simple. If they weigh more than 28 pounds, they can be disqualified from AKC competition. This does not prevent a 29 (or more) pound Frenchie from being a wonderful pet; he's just not a show dog.

Substance
Muscular, heavy bone.

Frenchies should give the appearance of being in great shape—

There's a lot of dog in this little frame.

not fat, but very muscular and stocky. "Heavy bone" refers to the thickness and density of the bones. Part of what makes a Frenchie unique is this solid, dense body type.

Head
Head large and square.

A French Bulldog should have a big, boxy head. He should look like a square when viewed from the front. This is very apparent when seeing a fine-quality French Bulldog.

Eyes
Dark in color, wide apart set low down in the skull, as far from the ears as possible, round in form, of moderate size, neither sunken or bulging, in lighter colored dogs, lighter colored eyes are acceptable. No haw and no white of the eye showing when looking forward.

The ideal Frenchie eye is a deep, dark chocolate, almost black. Cream-colored dogs may have a slightly lighter eye, but a yellow or golden eye is very, very undesirable. Slightly lighter means a brown one shade lighter, *not* several shades lighter. The correct Frenchie eye gives an appealing, baby-faced look to the Frenchie face. The eyes should never bulge or look "buggy." The haw (the third eyelid that is in the inside corner of the eye) should not be visible.

Everyone loves those adorable Frenchie ears!

Ears

Known as bat ear, broad at the base, elongated, with round top; set high on the head but not too close together and carried erect with the orifice to the front. The leather of the ear is fine and soft. Other than a bat ear is a disqualification.

Ah, the Frenchie ear! No other breed has the distinctive bat ear of the French Bulldog. This is one of the key characteristics of the breed, and correct ear placement is vital to the correct Frenchie appearance. The ears should never be low set or hang down. They should be set at approximately "eleven and one" to give that wonderful, alert expression. When the ears are low, the Frenchie loses the alert, mischievous expression required by the standard. A happy Frenchie with ears carried high is a joy to see.

Head

The top of the skull is flat between the ears; the forehead is not flat but slightly rounded. The muzzle broad, deep and well laid back; the muscles of the cheeks well developed. The stop well defined, causing a hollow groove between the eyes with heavy wrinkles forming a soft roll over the extremely short nose; nostrils broad with a distinct line between them. Nose black. Nose other than black is a disqualification. Except in the case of lighter colored dogs, where a lighter colored nose is acceptable, but not desirable.

The above section is critically important in defining the essence of a French Bulldog. The skull should be level between the ears, but the forehead is rounded. This also contributes to that delightful baby-faced look. The muzzle should be almost as wide as the head itself and full in appearance. Under the eyes should also be full and not "lack fill." "Plush" is the word that describes a correct Frenchie face. Over the very short nose should be a deep nose wrinkle. This nose wrinkle may take some time to develop fully. Some lines can have an open-faced look as teenagers and then develop the plush, prized face. The lighter nose is allowed in the cream and lighter fawn-colored dogs. The lighter nose is not a dudley or pink nose but more of a gray color. The nose should be not be a flesh tone or liver brown.

Frenchies are known for their boxy heads and dark eyes.

Neck, Topline, Body
The neck is thick and well arched with loose skin at the throat. The body is short and well rounded. The chest is broad, deep and full; well ribbed with the belly tucked up. The tail is either straight or screwed (but not curly), short, hung low, thick root and fine tip; carried low in repose.

A beautiful, arched neck can be what separates a good show dog from a great one. The Frenchie should have a front-heavy appearance when viewed from above. Many breeders describe it as a pear-shaped physique. As you would expect, the dog should have a deep, round chest with good, round spring of rib, almost barrel chested. "Tucked up" refers to the waist when viewed from the side; the Frenchie should curve up after the ribs. Tails should be short and close to the body, a little nub of a tail. It should not stick out or up and should be an extension of the spine. The tail should not be noticed; if it is, it is probably too big, too

long or improperly set. The tail can wag, and it is
delightful to see a happy French Bulldog wagging his
tiny tail.

Coat

*Coat is moderately fine, brilliant, short and smooth. Skin is
soft and loose, especially at the head and shoulders, forming
wrinkles.*

*It is normal for
your Frenchie to
have some wrin-
kling around
his neck and
shoulders.*

A Frenchie's coat will not be silky soft, but it will not be
coarse or harsh either. A French Bulldog will not be
overly wrinkled like a Chinese Shar-Pei, but there will
be some gentle wrinkling at the neck and shoulders.

Color Acceptable colors include all brindle, fawn, white,
brindle and white and any other
color except those that constitute
a disqualification. All colors are
acceptable with the exception of
solid black, mouse, liver, black
and tan, black and white and
white and black, which are dis-
qualifications. Black means black
without a trace of brindle.

*This photo
proves that there
are many differ-
ent types of
Frenchies from
which to choose.*

The color section of the standard is probably debated
more than any other, except possibly the weight
disqualification. Brindle refers to a pattern. Brindle

patterns can range from a virtually black Frenchie with a few red or brown hairs to a chocolate or red-based color covered with stripes of another color (like a tiger) from head to toe. Fawn can range from an off-white cream color to a deep mahogany red with all shades of gold in between. The pied color is actually white with spots of brindle (in any of the patterns) or fawn (in any of the colors noted above). The disqualifying colors have been debated for many years; there is much controversy over whether there ever was a mouse or liver Frenchie! The color should be the least of anyone's concerns. The health, temperament and soundness of the French Bulldog are the most important factors. It is thought that the disqualifying colors resulted from breeders wanting to distance the Frenchie from the bull-baiting and terrier ancestors of many years ago.

French Bulldogs are a playful, good-tempered breed.

Temperament

Well behaved, adaptable and comfortable companions with an affectionate nature and even disposition; generally active, alert and playful, but not unduly boisterous.

What a wonderful description of a lovely companion breed. The French Bulldog should epitomize just that . . . a happy companion.

Disqualifications

- Any alteration other than the removal of dewclaws

- Over 28 pounds in weight

- Other than bat ears

- Nose other than black, except in the case of lighter colored dogs, where a lighter color is acceptable

- Solid black (black without a trace of brindle), mouse, liver, black and tan

Could this be the next Miss America?

Pet vs. Show Dog

A pet French Bulldog will not meet all the points of the standard—not even the show dogs do that! But he should be immediately identifiable as a French Bulldog and should meet most of the points above. Often a nuance of the standard is the only reason a companion dog cannot become a show dog. A few teeth may show in the front, or he may be a little longer in the loin or a smidgen bigger than desired. But that does not prevent him from being a wonderful, healthy pet and a vital part of a family. I often tell people that I would never have won the Miss America pageant, but I am still identifiable as a person.

The
French Bulldog's
History

As you would expect, the French Bulldog is a descendant of the Bulldog. Toy Bulldog fanciers in England during the early 1800s developed a tiny, miniature Bulldog. Often weighing little more than 10 pounds, they were favored by many. By 1860, the Toy Bulldogs were even being shown in competition at dog shows.

With the Industrial Revolution came change, even for breeds of dogs. Many lace workers were forced out of work by the advent of machines that could make lace, and they had to look elsewhere for jobs. By the mid-1800s, many English lace workers emigrated to France and took their Toy Bulldogs with them. There they crossed the little Bulldogs with Pugs and different types of terriers. Thus began the French Bulldog as we know it today. The type was very different from today's Frenchie. They would be considered coarse by today's standards, and they varied widely in appearance. Some had rose ears (like a Bulldog), some had erect ears, some even had docked ears. Tails and leg length also varied widely.These little dogs caught the fancy of the French, and the demand for them skyrocketed. The *Bouledogues Francais*, as they were called in France, became the darling of the streetwalkers of that time. As often happens, fashion travels from the streets to high society, and the French Bulldog became all the rage among France's elite. A French Bulldog was a much-prized status symbol of the time. To accommodate the need for more of the little dogs, breeders crossed Pugs and terriers with the

Sacre bleu! It's easy to see why the French fell in love with this adorable breed.

Toy Bulldogs. Their characteristics are evident in the softer, rounder eye of the Pug and the more alert attitude of the terriers. Many Frenchies to this day are excellent mousers.

A ROYAL FRENCHIE

A French Bulldog, Ortino, was the beloved pet of Princess Tatiana of the Russian Imperial family. He was executed with the royal family June 16, 1918. Recently, when the mass grave containing the remains of this execution was unearthed, the skeleton of the little Frenchie was found with the bones of the Romanovs.

The French were, as a rule, rather nonchalant in their record keeping of pedigrees and such, so there is a lack of information from this time in Frenchie history.

French Bulldogs in the United States

As expected, affluent Americans were quick to fall in love with the charms of this whimsical little dog. Wealthy American tourists brought these delightful dogs back to the United States, where notable breeders of the time quickly set about the task of refining and defining the breed. Americans are universally regarded as having developed and standardized the bat ear in the French Bulldog. Americans also wrote the first breed standard and demanded American Kennel Club recognition.

French Bulldogs were first shown at the Westminster Kennel Club show in 1896, even though it was for exhibition only because they were not an accepted breed. In 1897, the French Bulldog Club of America was founded, and Walter W. Watrous was elected president. That year, the first sanctioned French Bulldog Specialty show was held at the Waldorf-Astoria Hotel in New York City. This show was written about in all the society columns and was one of the very first specialty shows, of any breed to be held in such posh circumstances. Society was fascinated by the little dogs, and immense popularity followed.

> **THE TITANIC FRENCHIE**
>
> A French Bulldog was one of the victims of the sinking of the *Titanic*. Wealthy American tycoon, Mr. Robert W. Daniels, had purchased a brindle male Gamin descendent in France and was bringing him back to New York to infuse new blood into the French Bulldogs in the United States. Unfortunately, the little French Bulldog drowned with hundreds of other victims, human and canine. Daniels survived the disaster and then sued for, and won, the then astronomical amount of $750 for the replacement cost of his beloved new pet.

Shortly after the turn of the century, the French Bulldog was the fifth most popular dog in America. There were exactly 100 entered at the Westminster Kennel Club show in 1906. Rockefellers, Morgans, Faulkners and many more prominent people of the day owned French Bulldogs. They were the darlings of society, with some selling for the then unheard-of amount of $3,000.

Americans soon caught the "Frenchie bug."

Then, in 1905, Samuel Goldenberg imported Nellcote Gamin from France. Gamin is credited with influencing the breed more dramatically than any other French Bulldog. He was considered the closest French Bulldog to the standard alive. He was virtually undefeated in the show ring and made his mark as a stud dog many times over. Gamin will be found in the pedigrees of most American French Bulldogs. Thus began the "Era of Gamin."

A continuous core of admirers kept the breed alive and quietly flourishing during the next fifty years or so. It has only been within the last ten to fifteen years that French Bulldogs have begun to steadily increase in numbers.

FAMOUS OWNERS OF FRENCH BULLDOGS

Jason Priestly

Jonathan Kellerman

King Edward VII

D.H. Lawrence

Elizabeth McGovern

Patty Hearst

Paul Winfield

Frau Ann Marie Sacher

Dorothy Parker

Colette

Toulouse Lautrec

The French Bulldog Club of America

The FBDCA has changed from a very elitist core of East Coast devotees to a nationwide club with members from virtually every state. The primary function of the FBDCA is to act as guardian of the breed standard. The FBDCA also sponsors an annual national specialty show, an active rescue organization and ongoing educational events.

Champion Ralanda Ami Francine, owned by Amanda West and handled by Jerry Rigden, won an amazing fifty-five Best in Show honors in the 1950s and 1960s.

French Bulldogs in Print and on the Silver Screen

French Bulldogs regularly appear in glossy magazines such as *Vogue*, *Harper's Bazaar*, *Polo*, *People* and even *GQ*.

A brindle French Bulldog was seen in the mega-hit movie *Titanic,* and one was actually lost in that fateful shipwreck. Little Frankie was the star (at least to Frenchie fans) of the recent action movie, *Armageddon.* Those with eagle Frenchie-spotting eyes saw a cream Frenchie in the Val Kilmer movie *At First Sight.*

So far, French Bulldogs have not suffered the same overexposure as the Chihuahua, the St. Bernard or the Dalmatian. We enjoy seeing our beloved breed in movies and magazines, but a glimpse is enough.

How Popularity Can Be Negative

Anytime a breed is overexposed and becomes the darling of the day, indiscriminate overbreeding can unfortunately occur. There are unscrupulous breeders that do not have the best interests of the breed at heart and will breed simply to sell puppies. Chapter 4 goes into more detail on selecting a reputable breeder.

It's wonderful that Frenchies are popular—as long as they don't become too popular.

Fortunately, French Bulldogs do not lend themselves to rapid overpopulation. Most French Bulldogs are artificially inseminated (bred), and virtually all French Bulldog puppies are born by Cesarean section. Also, litter sizes are usually small compared to other breeds of dogs. All these factors combined do not make for a "quick-buck" breed of dog.

Breeding and owning dogs is a very big responsibility. Dog ownership is a commitment that should not be taken lightly; owning a dog should be for the life of the dog. Do your homework and make your decision carefully.

chapter 3

The **World** According to the **French Bulldog**

"A true companion dog" is how many people describe French Bulldogs. Most breeds of dogs were bred for a specific function—hunting birds, tracking, herding cattle and the list goes on. But the little French Bulldog was bred simply to be a companion, and that is what he does best.

French Bulldogs are a very unique breed and they are definitely *not* for everyone. But, when you click with a Frenchie, it can be one of the most wonderful relationships that you can have with a dog.

21

Just like people, Frenchies have their own unique personalities and quirks. When a Frenchie becomes part of your life, you will never be the same. Just as a word of warning, it is hard to stop at just one. Some people describe them as being similar to potato chips; it is just too easy to want another one.

Frenchies and People

As you would expect, a dog bred to be a companion thrives on human companionship. No French Bulldog should ever be relegated to the life of an outside dog or a kennel dog. They must have daily interaction with the people in their lives, or they will not be fulfilled.

If a French Bulldog is already part of your life, you know how much he enjoys people. I often laugh that my Frenchies have absolutely no loyalty; they will go to anyone that will love them. This is great for the Frenchie in case he has to go to a new home later in life; he will rebond within days. It's not so great, however, for my ego!

Frenchies love to spend time with their humans.

French Bulldogs make wonderful therapy dogs, and many visit hospitals, nursing homes and hostels all over the country. Their compact size, neat coat and expressive faces make them big favorites. Frenchies seem to know that being with the elderly is not a time for boisterous play or activity. Some years ago, I visited my grandmother, then 95, now deceased. Whenever we could not find my little Joker, he would always be in my "Meemaw's" room sitting quietly beside her. One time, he had his paw protectively across her arm as he snuggled next to her.

CHILDREN AND FRENCHIES

People often ask, "How are Frenchies with children?" I reply, "How are your children with dogs?" Frenchies will take a lot of poking and prodding, but they are not Golden Retrievers. At some point, they will try to get away from the children. To be fair to both the dog and the children, do not leave the dog unattended with young children. Of course, you should never leave a toddler unattended with a dog of any breed.

This baby girl makes a fascinating new toy for her Frenchie.

Personally, I would not recommend bringing a puppy into a home with children under the age of 3. Housetraining a puppy and having a child in diapers would be too much for most of us mere mortals! This is, of course, a generalization, and your household might be perfectly ready for the challenge.

The playful side of this French Bulldog comes out whenever he pals around with his human friends.

It is often the dog that suffers when a new baby comes along. The Frenchie has been the center of the universe, and then all of a sudden here is this new, smelly, crying baby that gets all the attention. It is wise to introduce the baby and the dog carefully. Be very aware of your Frenchie's needs during this transition time. Be sure he is still getting plenty of attention and does not feel left out.

Of course, if for any reason your Frenchie and your child do not get along after all efforts have been exhausted to ensure that they do, then you must responsibly find the Frenchie a new home. Contact the breeder and explain the situation to her. Reputable breeders should take the dog back and find him a new home. If for some reason, the breeder is unable to rehome the Frenchie, you should contact French Bulldog rescue through the French Bulldog Club of America. There is information available and procedures are in place for just this type of situation. This should not be a course of action to be taken lightly. Bringing a pet into your home is a lifelong commitment and should be treated as such.

Life with a Frenchie

Dogs crave routine. Most tend to wake up and go to bed at about the same time every day. Mealtime, walk time and playtime should be at approximately the

same time every day. This includes weekends. By keeping to a more regular schedule, your Frenchie will become housetrained more easily and will be more secure and relaxed in general. My dogs seem to know that when the weather is over on the news, it

It's possible that your French Bulldog may snore.

is almost time to go to sleep. At around 10:30 every night, they get up and go to the back door for that last potty break.

I try to feed my dogs right before dark so that everybody has a full tummy before they go to bed. Daylight saving time presents a challenge twice a year. In anticipation of the switch, I start moving up (or back, depending on the time of the year) their dinnertime about two weeks before the switch. This helps keep them on a more regular routine.

Do They Snore?

This is one of the most often asked questions about Frenchies. And yes, some of them do. I have known Frenchies that sounded like a chain saw when they slept and others that did not snore a bit. Somewhat like people, right?

This brings us to where a Frenchie should sleep. This is a matter of personal preference. Many Frenchies seem to quickly find their way onto the bed, and that is where they sleep their entire lives. If this is not an option for whatever reason, other arrangements must be made.

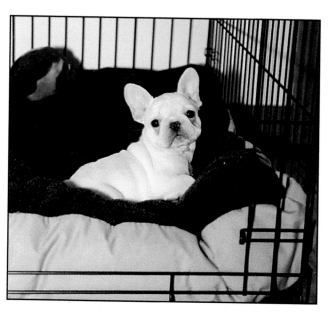

Even though he may rather sleep with you, your Frenchie will be just fine in his own bed at night as long as he is in a quiet place with a comfortable temperature.

If you choose to crate your French Bulldog for bedtime, you must decide where you want the crate to be. I would recommend the bedroom; even being in a crate in the same room with the owner is reassuring to

25

a dog, especially a puppy. But if that is not possible, a quiet spot is desired, possibly in the kitchen or laundry room. Just make sure the room is warm in the winter and cool in the summer.

WHAT WAS THAT?

Yes, this subject must be addressed. Some Frenchies have a tendency to be "gassy." A change in diet may help alleviate this condition, and there are supplements that can be added to their food. Check with your pet store or veterinarian for the availability of these products. Sometimes individual Frenchies just seem to have more flatulence than others. You have been forewarned.

Housetraining

The key to successful housetraining is an early start.

Frenchies can be a bit stubborn when it comes to housetraining, but be patient. They *will* catch on. It will take patience, perseverance, attention and lots of paper towels, but they will eventually become housetrained. Some individual dogs take longer than others, so just have faith. It can be frustrating and disheartening at times but stick with it.

Start housetraining *immediately!* Decide whether your dog will be paper trained or trained to go outside and then stick with that method. Get him on a regular feeding schedule and make plenty of trips outside. When the puppy runs around like he is looking for something—he is! Take him outside immediately (or to the paper). Upon waking from sleep, right after eating and anytime you just get home, take him out or to his paper. Also do this right before you go to bed.

26

Dogs should have unlimited access to fresh water at all times. It may be tempting to keep water from a puppy who is not yet housetrained, but that is not the right way to housebreak him. Puppies need water to develop properly. A regular feeding schedule will allow you to take him outside (or to paper) before and after eating. Most puppies will eliminate immediately upon waking up and after eating. Make it easier for everyone and work with your puppy on this schedule.

Keep in mind that accidents *will* happen. If you catch him right in the *middle* of the act, rush him outside (or to his paper). It does *no* good to rub his nose in it (an old, mean wives' tale). Do not yell at him when you discover a mess; he will not understand why you are angry. He will just learn to hide when you come home, expecting you to yell at him. Also, do not use ammonia-based cleaners to clean the mess; they smell like urine to dogs. Purchase a special cleaner designed to eliminate pet odors.

Keeping a similar routine every day helps the housetraining process along.

There are also "puppy pads" that are helpful in housebreaking your puppy. They have a plastic backing that will help protect your floors from urine. Find a place that is easily accessible for your puppy, easy for you to clean, and not in a high traffice area of the house for the "potty place," if you have chosen to paper train. Then place the puppy pad or newspaper in the selected area. I have found it helpful to use a little bit of the previously soiled newspaper as a reminder of where to go. Much like us, dogs are creatures of habit and your puppy will find a place that suits *her* if you do not select a place for her to "go" first. Housebreaking your puppy can be the most challenging part of having a new dog and if it is dealt with efficiently and quickly, everyone's life will be easier.

Every Frenchie has his own rate of learning, but even the most stubborn Frenchie should be pretty reliable by 4 to 5 months of age. I have had great success since I installed a doggy door, and my Frenchies can come and go at will. If this is an option, it may be your best bet.

Frenchies and the Great Outdoors

French Bulldogs are a brachycephalic breed. This means they have short, flat faces and very short noses. It is very easy for a Frenchie to overheat quickly with deadly results. Do not ever, ever leave your French Bulldog in a parked car if the temperature is over 70°F—your return could be delayed for reasons out of your control. The car will act as an oven with possibly fatal results. Please do not think, "It is only for a minute." I leave my Frenchies home in the air-conditioning (except for essential trips) in the hot summer months.

Romping in the snow can be great fun for your French Bulldogs! Be careful not to leave them outside too long, however, as their short coats do not provide much warmth.

They can also overheat outside, especially when it is humid. During hot months, keep your Frenchie inside except for brief supervised visits outside. If you do not have air-conditioning, have a fan and plenty of cool water for them. I keep kiddie-type swimming pools half-filled with water in the backyard all summer for my Frenchies to play in. It is interesting to watch the older Frenchies teach the puppies how to use the swimming pool to cool off. They get in and lie down, submerging themselves up to their eyes like little bat-eared hippos. It is so intriguing that the puppies have to give it a try.

I moved to Minnesota several years ago after more than twenty years in Texas. Believe it or not, my French Bulldogs love the cooler weather and actually are quite the little snow bunnies. I have benches in the backyard, and they will sit on them and "sun" when it is only in the thirties. They will go out after a fresh snowfall and dig tunnels throughout the yard. I will only see the tips of their ears as they bound through the drifts. However, they stay out only as long as they want and can come in the minute it is not fun anymore. Doggy doors are great for this time of the year! Mine do not wear sweaters or coats, but many French Bulldogs do appreciate the extra warmth of a little sweater.

Note: Be sure to use a pet-safe product when you de-ice. The regular products will burn and injure their feet. Your pet store should have a safe de-icing product.

You should also occasionally check their feet for burrs or thorns, even if they are not limping. Dogs that play outside a lot should be examined, not just for fleas and ticks, but for other things that can irritate them.

Your Frenchie will adore playing outside with you as long as you keep his short legs in mind. He may not last as long as you do!

It is a sad fact of life that dogs are not always safe unattended, even in their own backyards. Unfortunately, there are many cases of French Bulldogs being stolen from the supposed security of their own homes. No one can be expected to watch their dog twenty-four hours a day, but if you live in an area that might require extra vigilance, I suggest that you do not leave your beloved Frenchie alone outside. You may consider having a six foot tall privacy fence installed, instead of see-through chain link. Many people have installed a smaller "dog run" within the security of their fenced yard. This allows your Frenchie to enjoy extra time outside without constant human supervision. This enclosure can also be used just for potty breaks and will limit your clean-up area.

A DOG'S SENSES

Sight: With their eyes located farther apart than ours, dogs can detect movement at a greater distance than we can, but they can't see as well up close. They can also see better in less light but can't distinguish many colors.

Sound: Dogs can hear about four times better than we can, and they can hear high-pitched sounds especially well. Their ancestors, the wolves, howled to let other wolves know where they were; our dogs do the same, but they have a wider range of vocalizations including barks, whimpers, moans and whines.

Smell: A dog's nose is his greatest sensory organ. His sense of smell is so great he can follow a trail that's weeks old, can detect odors diluted to one-millionth the concentration we'd need to notice them and can even sniff out a person underwater!

Taste: Dogs have fewer taste buds than we do, so they're likelier to try anything—and usually do—which is why it's especially important for their owners to monitor their food intake. Dogs are omnivores, which means they eat meat as well as vegetable matter like grasses and weeds.

Touch: Dogs are social animals and love to be petted, groomed and played with.

Potential "dognapping" is another good reason to microchip your dog. A friend of mine had a French Bulldog stolen from her home by the pool cleaner. Over a year later, she was recovered and it was proven that she belonged to her lawful owner because she had a microchip. Litigation was successful against the thief, in case you wondered! I am always cautious when strangers seem overly interested in my Frenchies and ask too many questions about cost, rarity, etc. I downplay the rarity of the breed and never discuss price or anything to do with money with strangers. Unfortunately, many breeders are no longer using their physical addresses in advertisements, as unscrupulous people have posed as puppy buyers, only to come back later and steal the puppies! I know breeders that insist upon meeting away from their home/kennel for the initial visit with prospective puppy buyers. This is a very sad state of affairs. So, do not be offended if a breeders seems a bit overly cautious; this problem could be the reason.

Frenchies will enjoy running and playing outside, but they are not built for long jogs and intense exercise. A brisk walk will be good for both of you. Just remember, your Frenchie has very short little legs!

Frenchies and Other Animal Friends

Most Frenchies will get along famously with other dogs and even cats (especially if they are raised together). Sometimes you will encounter a Frenchie that does not care for other dogs; in this case, it is best to listen to what he is telling you. Do not force him to "play nice" with other dogs. Maybe your Frenchie is a bit of a loner and prefers your company to that of other dogs.

The tough little Frenchman does not always realize he is a small dog (don't tell him I said so) and may not behave appropriately around much bigger dogs. Most big dogs are benevolent enough to ignore a little 20-something pound Frenchie, but some are not. Exercise caution when introducing your Frenchie to other playmates of all sizes!

Familiarity with cats from an early age will help your Frenchie get along with other furry friends.

In my own experience, Frenchies do well with cats if they are familiar with cats their entire life. A friend of mine has a female Frenchie, Allis, that actually nursed a litter of orphan kittens and raised them as her own. To this day, the kittens think of Allis as mom.

On the Go with Your Frenchie

Get your Frenchie used to traveling with you by taking him for frequent short trips. Even though we all love our veterinarians, do *not* make the only time he gets to ride in the car a trip to the veterinarian!

Do not travel with your Frenchie when he has a full stomach—I do not think I need to elaborate! Before any car trip, take him for a little walk. This will allow him to use the bathroom, if necessary, and will possibly tire him enough to go right to sleep. We all love to have our buddy on the seat next to us, but he really is safer traveling in a crate or in a secure pet seat belt. Accidents do happen. Your beloved pet will be much safer in a crate in the event of something unforeseen. Always have a collar and lead for when you stop. Keep him on the lead at all times. If possible, have two tags on him, one with your permanent address and one stating where you can be reached while on your trip. There are tags available that have little slips of paper in a tube so you can change the information as often as needed.

These two little guys are ready to roll.

If you are on a long car trip, stop every four to five hours. Frenchies need more frequent stops than we do. Be a good neighbor—pick up what your Frenchie leaves. Keep a box of plastic sandwich bags in your automobile for this purpose. Take your own dog food for him and, if possible, water since changes can upset Frenchie tummies.

If you are flying with your Frenchie, check with your airline for particulars on health certificates, crates, vaccinations and more. Hopefully, he will be able to ride in the cabin in an airline-approved pet carrier bag. There are many available that look like soft-sided luggage. If not, make sure you are on direct nonstop flights during cooler times of the day. If in doubt about the temperature, do not take your Frenchie. No trip is worth jeopardizing his life. Make the airline inform you that your dog has been loaded on the plane. Do not hesitate to be forceful—this is your darling we are talking about!

Ensure that any hotels/motels you are staying at will accept dogs; some do not. Be considerate of others in the motel. Do not leave him unattended in the room if you think he might bark. I am always careful to walk my dogs well away from the hotel and to pick up after them every single time.

Take extra precautions about the safety of his travel crate and the temperature when you are traveling with your Frenchie.

For international travel, check with your veterinarian. Each country is different and will have dramatically different rules and regulations regarding traveling with your pet.

Have fun! You are traveling with your best friend.

IF YOUR FRENCHIE CAN'T GO WITH YOU

In the event that you must go on a trip and your Frenchie cannot go with you, think about what is best for him. You might want to consider having a pet sitter come to your home to feed and play with him a specified number of times a day. There are many reputable, bonded pet sitters in virtually every area of the country. Ask your veterinarian for a referral or check the Yellow Pages. During the

interview, if you are not 100-percent comfortable with the pet sitter, thank him for his time and select another sitter.

A boarding kennel may be an option for you. Once again, check with your veterinarian for referrals. You should visit the boarding kennel and make sure it is up to the standards your Frenchie deserves. A good boarding kennel with be heated, air-conditioned, clean and well-lit with a pleasant odor. Check with each kennel about requirements for vaccinations, food (some ask you to bring your own food, other do not) and check-in and checkout times.

Of course, if you have a reliable friend or relative that is willing to stop by twice a day (or more) and check on and play with your

The ideal pet sitter is someone who makes your Frenchie feel as comfortable as you do.

Frenchie, that can be a wonderful option. Be sure that you leave all contact numbers for them, just in case. Remember to include the regular veterinarian, emergency (after hours) veterinarian and possible numbers of other "French Bulldog friends" that can answer questions for them, if necessary.

More French Bulldog Information

BOOKS

Eltinge, S. and Dr. J. Grebe. *The Flat Face Encyclopedia: A to Z on Bulldogs and French Bulldogs.* Mendota, MN: ArDesign Inc., 1997.

Grebe, Dr. J. *Healthy Frenchies: An Owner's Manual.* Mendota, MN: ArDesign, Inc., 1998.

Toye, A. *The French Bulldog Pocket Handbook.* Mendota, MN: ArDesign, Inc., 1999.

National Breed Club

The French Bulldog Club of America
Vicki Kerr, Secretary
566 Ravine Dr.
Valparaiso, IN 46385
www.frenchbulldog.org/fbdca

Magazines

The French Bullytin
P.O. Box 50680
Mendota, MN 55150
Phone: 651-454-9510
Fax: 651-454-9460
www.ardesigninc.com

Award-winning, full-color, quarterly magazine. An excellent source for up-to-date information on the breed.

Other Sources

www.frenchbulldog.org

Comprehensive Web site with more than 300 pages of information and links to other sites, breeders, Frenchie history and much more.

www.frenchbulldogs.org

Excellent site with links to breeders, other French Bulldog–related sites and various breeding and dog show information.

www.ardesigninc.com

Fun site with lots of information and pictures of French Bulldogs, breeders, articles and more.

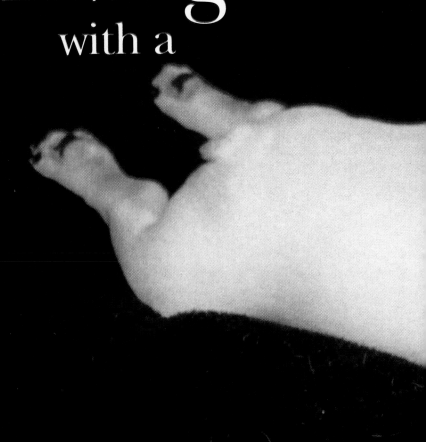

Living
with a

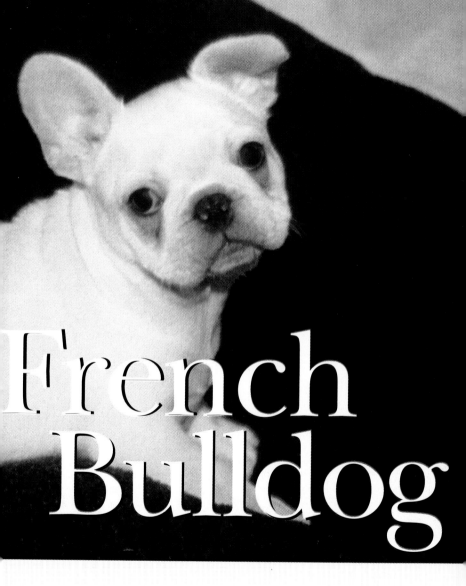

part two

French Bulldog

chapter 4

Bringing **Home** Your French Bulldog

Purchasing a dog is a lifetime commitment. Do not bring a dog into your life if it is a higher-than-normal stress time, if you are about to move, or if you are expecting a baby or have some other impending major event. If a perfectly immaculate house is of utmost importance to you, you might not want to get a Frenchie or any dog for that matter. Be realistic—is a dog right for you at this time in your life? Your Frenchie deserves your full attention and commitment, especially at the beginning and especially if you are getting a puppy!

First Things First

Do you want a puppy? Would an older puppy or an adult be right for you? When it comes to French Bulldogs, it is not critical to get a puppy to have a bonded companion. As mentioned before, Frenchies rebond very easily and adjust to new situations quickly. If you decide that an older puppy or even an adult is right for your situation, there may be a few more options available to you. Occasionally, rescue Frenchies are available. Thankfully, this is not a common occurrence, but it does happen. These dogs may require extra work on your part. They might have socialization or housetraining issues. Be prepared for a little more patience and effort, especially when a rescued dog first comes into your home. Breeders might also have an older puppy that, for whatever reason, is not going to be used in a breeding program or is not destined to be a show dog. This will not make her a less desirable pet; she's just not a show dog! Breeders might even have retired show dogs that make wonderful pets and friends. A breeder that shares a retired champion is not being heartless, he is just allowing the retired dog to be someone's special dog, not just one of several.

It is not necessary to start with a French Bulldog puppy to develop a special bond between you and your pet. Older Frenchies can develop attachments to you just as easily, and probably won't need housetraining!

Be sure you have done your homework. Frenchies are a relatively uncommon breed, and you will probably not see them in your local newspaper ads. You might be on a waiting list for a puppy for quite some time. You might even purchase your puppy sight unseen and have her shipped to you. There are many reputable breeders that truly have the best interests of the breed at heart, but unfortunately, many are just out to make money. You must carefully select the breeder of your future family member.

There are several ways to begin. You may contact the American Kennel Club for a list of breeders in your area (or the entire country). Your local kennel club (most areas have one or more) should be able to refer you to local breeders. Ask your veterinarian or, if you do not have a veterinarian, call several in your area and ask if they have any French Bulldogs among their clientele. This will give you a head start on selecting a veterinarian that is familiar with the unique needs of this breed. There are also breed magazines that list breeders in the classified sections, so make some calls. More and more breeders are now going online. The Internet can be a wonderful tool to help in your search, but just like other methods, it has drawbacks. Anyone can say virtually anything he or she wants to on the Internet, so surfer beware.

Now the tough part begins. You will want to interview the breeders carefully. Here is a partial list of things you might look for in a responsible breeder:

- Is he a member of the French Bulldog Club of America (not all good breeders are members, but it is a start) or local all-breed kennel clubs?

- Does he show his dogs in AKC competitions or have them shown? Most reputable breeders want to compare their dogs to other breeders' dogs and do compete. A champion title is not necessarily a mark of a good dog, but it shows that an effort has been made. Along these lines, do not be dazzled by lots of champions in the pedigree; Frenchies are relatively easy to put a champion title on. But if there are very few champions in the pedigree, that should be a caution sign. Once again, most reputable Frenchie breeders do show their dogs.

- Is he willing to provide a written guarantee on the health of the puppy? As with any purebred dog, there are certain conditions to which the French Bulldog is genetically predisposed, but the breeder should guarantee against life-threatening inherited conditions. Keep in mind that no one can predict the future, and no breeder, no matter how reputable, can guarantee that every puppy sold will be problem-free her entire life!

- Is he willing to provide references from other puppy buyers?

- Are the puppies at least started on their series of puppy shots and have they been wormed? Will the breeder provide a health certificate from a veterinarian?

I tell people to listen to their gut instinct when talking to a breeder. If it does not feel right and something is bothering you, thank him for his time and say good-bye. A breeder should be willing to help you and answer your questions for the life of the dog.

Boy or Girl?

Male and female Frenchies make equally good pets. In my own personal experience, I have found that the boys cling to me a bit more, and the girls are more independent.

Both boy and girl puppies have something special to offer.

How Old?

Most Frenchies are somewhat slow to mature. My Frenchies do not go to their new homes until they are 10 to 12 weeks old at the very least. This ensures that they have been given at least two of their initial set of shots. An 8-week-old puppy is too immature to leave her mother and littermates. If a breeder pressures you to take a puppy at this age, consider it a red warning flag. I firmly believe that they learn how to be dogs and are much more secure Frenchies when they stay with mom a little bit longer. Plus, mom will teach them some dog manners!

Puppy-Proofing Your House

Having a puppy is like having a tiny toddler in the house. Everything will go in her mouth—electrical cords, pennies, shoes, chair legs and so on. Get down on the floor at your puppy's eye level—the world looks really different. Put those plastic electric-outlet protectors in each unused plug. Also, tie up electrical cords or block them from puppy's reach. Any house plants should be out of puppy's reach also. If there is a cat, keep the litter box where your new Frenchie does not have access to it.

A puppy should not have the run of the house, especially when she is learning to be housetrained. Usually, the kitchen is the best choice for a place to keep your new Frenchie when you are not there. Floors can easily be mopped, and we all know the mop will be out in full force until your Frenchie is housetrained. I strongly suggest using a doggy gate to contain the puppy in the kitchen. This allows the puppy to see out and to feel a part of things. Even if there is a door, the doggy/baby gate is a better option. I recommend that you get the plastic, pressure-fitted, mesh type. It is preferable to the wooden slatted type. A puppy can get her head stuck in the wooden slats too easily!

Many people have had very good results using an exercise pen in the kitchen. Exercise pens are available at your pet-supply store or through pet-supply catalogs. Exercise pens, or X-pens as they are called, resemble

---

DANGERS TO YOUR FRENCHIE

INSIDE

Electrical cords

Cleaning supplies

Chocolate

House plants

Poisons (rat, mouse, insecticides and so on)

Medications and vitamins (human and dog)

Garbage in general (bones, glass, metal and so on)

OUTSIDE

Antifreeze

Poisons (rat, mouse, insecticides and so on)

Fertilizers

---

small portable fences and are found in a variety of sizes. I always set up an exercise pen with the puppy's food and water and a comfortable bed at one end and newspapers at the other. For Frenchies, I recommend the 30-inch height. You can easily reach over it and pick up your puppy, papers or whatever. If you have an escape artist on your hands, you may have to invest in a taller one.

If you do not have a securely fenced yard, you might want to invest in a small dog run. Dog run panels are available at home-supply stores and can provide your new Frenchie with a place to stretch her legs off-leash. This will allow you to pop her in there first thing in the morning to let her "take care of business" while you start that pot of coffee. Even dogs need a little privacy every now and then. If this is not an option, take your exercise pen outside to give her a chance to play in it. If you are an apartment dweller, the exercise pen can be taken to the park or your apartment's courtyard and be set up to give her some freedom.

PUPPY ESSENTIALS

Your new puppy will need the following items:

A food bowl

A water bowl

A collar

A leash

An ID tag

A bed

A crate

Toys

Grooming supplies

Supervising Your Frenchie

Especially when your puppy is small, keep an eye on her at all times. Just like a toddler, a puppy is a quick little being with mischief on her mind! It only takes a moment for a puppy to pull a lamp off a table and injure herself.

Supply Shopping!

You've done your homework, have decided that a Frenchie is the perfect breed for you, have developed a rapport with a reputable breeder and have decided on just the right French Bulldog to share your life with. Now is the time to go shopping and prepare for your puppy's arrival.

CRATES

A crate is a must-have. There are two basic types of crates: metal and plastic. Both have advantages and disadvantages. A metal crate is good for visibility; the puppy can see what is going on, and you can more easily see what she is doing. If you select a suitcase-style (collapsible) crate, you will be able to move it easily from room to room. If showing your Frenchie is in your plans, this type of crate is much easier to transport. Metal crates, however, cannot be used for airline travel without adaptation. They can also be drafty in colder weather.

A crate is not a punishment area—it's your Frenchie's personal escape from the world.

The plastic type of crate is required for airline travel. A plastic crate offers more warmth in winter and is more private for your dog. Plastic is also easier to clean, which is great for that beginning housetraining stage.

FOOD AND WATER BOWLS

Of course, you need to invest in high-quality food and water bowls that can be cleaned easily. There are many varieties on the market. Stainless steel will last a life-time and can be easily cleaned. Your pet-supply store or catalog should have just the ones for your new Frenchie. While you are there, do not forget a pooper scooper, a pretty self-explanatory item.

COLLARS AND LEADS

Collars come next. The inexpensive, smooth, nylon type in which the buckle makes its own hole in the collar is a good starter collar. Select one that is at least 2 inches longer than the puppy's neck so she will have growing room and you won't be buying a new collar every week. A thin matching lead will work to begin leash-training. Do not buy a collar and leash so heavy that your puppy is weighed down by them. When your Frenchie is approximately 9 or 10 months old, you should be able to select a permanent collar and lead. Frenchie necks are exceptionally thick, and if you have a male Frenchie, her neck may continue to grow

until she is 2 years or older. There are many stylish, durable collars and leads on the market; you can easily select a suitable one for your Frenchie. If you choose to use a choke-type collar on your Frenchie, remember to take it off when the leash comes off . . . no ifs, ands or buts. This type of collar can be good for training and walks, but it can be deadly if it catches on something. Your Frenchie could even get her jaw or foot caught in it and injure herself or worse.

Your Frenchie will soon get used to her collar and leash.

45

The retractable-type leash is great for giving your puppy freedom while keeping her under control. These leashes range in length from 10 feet to 26 feet.

BEDS

A suitable bed is the next necessity. For a growing, teething puppy, you do not want to invest in an expensive, designer-type bed; I also would steer away from beds that have exposed foam on the bottom. The temptation to flip the bed over and chew may be too great for your puppy! The thick, comfy lamb's wool–type beds work well. There is a variety of styles available from flat pads to donut-shaped beds in which Frenchies love to curl up. Most are warm, can easily be washed and stay good-looking for a long time. When teething and housetraining are over, you can invest in the designer dog bed of your dreams.

Qualities for a perfect Frenchie bed include warmth and durability.

TOYS

Now we'll move on to the most important category of all (at least to your Frenchie)—toys! There are literally hundreds, if not thousands, of dog toys available now. The ones I have recommended are based on ten years of experience in the pet industry and my own in-house panel of French Bulldog toy testers.

There are many types of hard nylon and rubber chew toys available now; many are chicken or liver flavored, and some even glow in the dark. I would recommend a large dog size for most Frenchies. Some types of therapeutic chew toys allow your Frenchie to chew while cleaning her teeth. There are raised tips on the toys that massage the gums while she chews.

There are also wonderful, cornstarch-based and plant-based bones that are completely digestible and odorless. It takes a couple weeks for a typical Frenchie to devour one of these medium-size bones.

French Bulldogs love toys, big or small. Toys supply a wonderful outlet for chewing energy.

Any of the sherpa, lamb's wool–type fleece toys or the fuzzy ones with the different sounds are always a big hit. These toys can be comforting to young puppies away from home for the first time. Keep an eye on your Frenchie to make sure she doesn't chew off an ear or an eye and swallow it.

I do not recommend pig ears or hooves for Frenchies. The ears get really soft and can easily get stuck in the dog's flat, French Bulldog throat, causing choking. The hooves can also break teeth and splinter. For the same reason, I do not recommend any type of rawhide chew.

Little latex squeak toys are allowed but only under supervision. Puppies love these toys but can tear them apart and can possibly swallow the squeaker or the latex.

Many experts recommend that you allow a puppy to have no more than three toys at a time. This keeps her from thinking that everything in the house is hers, and it also keeps her from becoming bored with her toys. I put the toys away for a while, and when I bring them back out, the dogs think they have all-new toys!

Having a new Frenchie puppy can be one of the most exciting times of all. With a little planning and shopping, you should be able to have a safe and happy homecoming for your new addition. But most importantly, have fun and enjoy each day with your new puppy—she won't stay a puppy for long!

I Have Questions—Help!

Your breeder should be willing to answer questions for the life of your dog. This is another reason it is so important to select a breeder with care. If for some reason the breeder is unavailable, contact another French Bulldog breeder and see if he is open to answering your questions.

For health questions, do not hesitate to consult your veterinarian. Your veterinarian may be able to suggest a specialist if he cannot answer your questions.

Selecting a Veterinarian

Your breeder may be able to recommend a good veterinarian in your area. If not, try to find out if there's a veterinarian in your area with expertise in treating the Bulldog breeds: Frenchies, Bulldogs, Pugs or Boston Terriers. The flat faces have their own unique set of needs when it comes to anesthesia and many procedures. Having a comfortable rapport with your veterinarian is essential. You must trust and respect your veterinarian. No matter how highly recommended a veterinarian is, if you do not enjoy your trips to see him, you need to select another one. Chapter 7 contains more information on selecting a veterinarian.

You will need to have your female Frenchie spayed before she comes into her first heat cycle to take advantage of the most health benefits. Her chances of having mammary or uterine cancer will be greatly reduced by having her spayed prior to her first heat cycle. You will also be spared the mood swings, mess and inconvenience of heat cycles.

To lessen your male Frenchie's "leg lifting," it is recommended that he be neutered before he begins marking territory. Your veterinarian will be able to provide more information on optimum times for neutering your dog. Neutering your male dog will have many benefits. He will be less aggressive toward other males, will have less desire to wander (looking for love), and will have a reduced chance of prostate cancer.

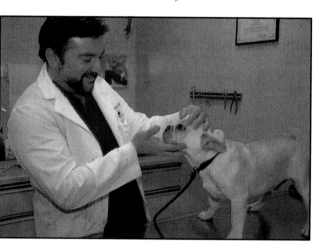

It is essential that both you and your French Bulldog have a good relationship with your veterinarian.

Reputable breeders will require that your pet Frenchie be spayed or neutered, and you will probably be given "limited" registration AKC papers. Your Frenchie will still be AKC registered; she's just unable to compete in AKC events, and her offspring would not be eligible for registration.

chapter 5

Feeding
Your French
Bulldog

A nutritious, balanced diet is essential to your Frenchie's health and well-being. There are many, many dog foods on the market, and it is up to you to select the food that is best for your dog.

Where to Go

I strongly recommend that you feed your Frenchie any of the premium brands of dog food. Our dogs do not have any choice in what they eat. They eat what we put in their bowl, so make it the very best food you can.

Pet-food superstores and pet stores carry a wide variety of premium pet foods. Your breeder might recommend a specific food, and if it is a premium food, you might wish to stick with that food. Your Frenchie is used to it and will have none of the stomach upsets that can occur when switching to a new food. If you are unable to continue to feed the recommended food for whatever reason, check with your veterinarian.

Why Buy a Premium Food?

Proper nutrition will help your new friend lead a long, healthy life. Your French Bulldog does not have a choice as to what he eats; his food will be what you provide, so make it a good choice. A bargain food may cost less, but it is no bargain in the long run. Premium foods guarantee that the ingredients will not vary from "batch to batch" as they can in bargain foods. The nutrition found in premium foods is consistent and properly balanced. This is called a "fixed-formula" food. With bargain foods, the ingredients can vary from bag to bag, depending on what ingredients were available at the best price at the time of manufacture. Plus, those cheaper ingredients can have varying degrees of digestibility. This can also cause stomach upsets and lapses in housebreaking.

The premium food may cost more per bag, but it will be more economical in the long run because your dog will get the nutrients he needs in less food, so he will eat less, which will offset the initial higher purchase price.

Premium foods will also have higher digestibility, which makes for a healthier coat and skin. In a short coated breed like a Frenchie, poor nutrition can be apparent in dry,

HOW TO READ THE DOG FOOD LABEL

How can you be sure you are feeding the right food to your dog? The information is all there on the label—if you know what you're looking for.

Look for the nutritional claim right at the top. Is the food "100 percent nutritionally complete"? If so, it's for nearly all life stages; "growth and maintenance" is for early development. Puppy foods and foods for senior dogs are specially marked so you can choose the proper food for your dog's stage.

Ingredients are listed in descending order by weight. The first three or four ingredients will tell you the bulk of what the food contains. Look for the highest-quality ingredients, like meats and grains, to be among them.

The Guaranteed Analysis tells you what levels of protein, fat, fiber and moisture are in the food, in that order. Although these numbers are meaningful, they won't tell you much about the quality of the food. The nutritional value is in the dry matter, not the moisture content.

In many ways, seeing is believing. If your dog has bright eyes, a shiny coat, a good appetite and a good energy level, chances are his diet's fine. Your dog's breeder and your veterinarian are good sources of advice if you're still not sure which food is appropriate.

brittle hair and a dull, dry appearance to the coat. A premium food with the proper balances of fatty acids can keep your Frenchie looking his best!

In summary, premium foods provide the following:

- High-quality ingredients
- High digestibility
- Well-balanced protein, fat, carbohydrate, vitamin and mineral levels
- Nutrient-packed formulas appropriate for each stage of your dog's life
- Consistent, stable ingredients
- Fatty-acid levels that do not change
- Excellent palatability (taste)
- Product guarantees
- Customer support

The benefits of a premium food are:

- Healthier skin and coat
- Healthier teeth and bones
- Better muscle tone
- Easier clean-up (less and firmer stool)
- Happy, healthy dog

Most premium foods even have puppy formulas specifically designed for the size of dog that you have. A French Bulldog usually falls right on the border between small and medium; I usually opt for the small breed formulas. If in doubt, consult your veterinarian.

What About the Raw Food Diets?

Yes, there has been a lot of publicity about all-natural raw diets. Some consist mostly of bones and raw meats, and others are homemade diets. Many experts are reluctant to recommend these diets for several reasons. First, it is virtually impossible for a person to be able to maintain consistency in a homemade diet. It would be a full-time job to try to duplicate what the dog food companies have done. Also, many raw diets have potentially harmful possibilities, such as bacterial infection or even e.coli. Many veterinarians have had dogs that experienced severe side effects from raw diets—nutritional imbalances, immune system problems and so on. In my personal opinion, we no longer have to eat the stomach contents of wildebeest to get our nutrition, so why should our dogs? If you are considering a raw diet, please consult your veterinarian and proceed with caution.

What Is in My Frenchie's Food?

A well-balanced diet will have five major food groups of nutrients: proteins, fats, carbohydrates, vitamins and minerals.

Feeding your Frenchie the best food will help him reach his potential in all realms of his life.

Proteins build and maintain your Frenchie's body tissues and help with growth. Fats provide energy and help maintain a glossy, healthy coat. Carbohydrates also provide energy in the form of calories and help promote digestion. Vitamins are vital for good vision, muscle tone, a healthy coat and more. Minerals aid in muscle development, build blood and provide strength to the bones. Don't forget that water also is necessary for your dog's health. All

Frenchies should have unlimited access to water at all times unless restricted by your veterinarian for a specific reason.

There are three types of dog food: dry, canned and semi-moist. The most common is dry food or kibble. Most veterinarians, trainers and breeders recommend that you feed a premium-quality dry food. It is convenient, easy to prepare and economical. Canned food is usually about 75 percent water and is not the most economical food type. Plus, feeding all-moist food will lead to looser stools and messier cleanup. The semi-moist foods are usually found in grocery stores, are the least economical and offer the fewest benefits nutritionally.

You may choose to add additional items to your dog's food such as pasta, rice or vegetables. This French Bulldog enjoys a dollop of cottage cheese mixed with his food.

I prefer to mix a little canned food in with the dry food. Add a little warm water and you have the best of both worlds—a palatable, nutritious food that Frenchies enjoy. Every day I also cook a little pasta, rice or some other starch and add it to their food. This is not really necessary, but it makes me feel I am doing something special for my "crew." Sometimes I mix a package of vegetables into their dinner or even give them each an entire carrot to enjoy. They each run to their own special spots to enjoy each and every bite of the carrot.

WHAT DO THE LABELS ON DOG FOOD PACKAGES MEAN?

There are five parts of most dog food labels. With a little understanding you can tell at a glance exactly what is in the food you are considering.

The name of the food is the first part. It tells you how much of an ingredient is actually in the food. For instance, if a food says *Chicken Formula*, it must be 25% chicken. If it says *with Chicken* or *Chicken Flavored*, that means that the food can be as little as 3% of that particular ingredient.

The ingredient panel is next. This is where you will find all the food sources that make up the product. The ingredients are listed in order according to weight before cooking. Make sure the first ingredient is always a high-quality meat protein, such as chicken, lamb or beef, but not ground corn. If a manufacturer is using a lot of vegetable protein (like soy) in its food, it may be to lower manufacturing costs.

Yummy! Your dog doesn't need a lot of variety to love his food. Dogs don't get bored with the same food every day the way we do.

There should also be a chart that lists the "guaranteed analysis" of the food. These figures show the content of the food and allow you another chance to compare protein and fat contents. Protein, fat, fiber and moisture contents should all be listed.

The Association of American Feed Control Officers (AAFCO) has statements that mean different things. If the statement say, "animal feeding tests using AAFCO procedures," then the food was fed to dogs at that life stage and it was found to be adequate. If it says, "meeting nutrient profiles," the dog food has not been tested on dogs; it was just analyzed in a laboratory and compared to charts.

The manufacturer's name and address are required to be on the bag of food. Many companies also list telephone numbers and Web site addresses. Companies that list a toll-free number usually welcome questions and telephone calls.

Life Stage Foods

You should always choose a food that is appropriate for your Frenchie's age and activity level. Your puppy should eat a premium puppy food until he is approximately 1 year old. After 1 year of age, your Frenchie will be ready to switch to an adult premium food, and then at approximately 8 years of age, it is time for senior food.

If you are switching your puppy from the food the breeder fed to another premium food, it should be done gradually. This will, hopefully, lessen or eliminate any stomach upsets caused by too abrupt of a switch. Usually, the first day you should mix 25% of the new food and 75% of the previous food. The second day, the ratio should be 50/50 of old food and new. On the third day, you can mix 25% old food and 75% new food, and on the fourth day, you can feed 100% new food. You can use this same schedule when it is time to switch him from puppy to adult food and then again from adult to senior food.

TO SUPPLEMENT OR NOT TO SUPPLEMENT?

If you're feeding your dog a diet that's correct for his developmental stage and he's alert, healthy-looking and neither over- nor underweight, you don't need to add supplements. These include table scraps as well as vitamins and minerals. In fact, unless you are a nutrition expert, using food supplements can actually hurt a growing puppy. For example, mixing too much calcium into your dog's food can lead to musculoskeletal disorders. Educating yourself about the quantity of vitamins and minerals your dog needs to be healthy will help you determine what needs to be supplemented. If you have any concerns about the nutritional quality of the food you're feeding, discuss them with your veterinarian.

Set a regular feeding schedule and stick to it. Your new puppy should have three small meals a day, preferably morning, noon and evening. If you are unable to feed him at lunch time, feed him his mixed food for breakfast and then leave a little dry food for him to munch on throughout the day. Personally, I do not like to have food or mealtime be the focus of a dog's life. That is why I leave food for my dogs to nibble on throughout the day. If they are not ravenous at mealtime, there are no scuffles in a multiple-dog household!

When your puppy is about 5 or 6 months old, you can eliminate the middle meal and just feed him breakfast and dinner. This should work well for his entire life.

If your Frenchie gains or loses weight, consult your veterinarian. You might need to feed him slightly smaller portions or switch to a reduced-calorie food. If he seems thin and needs to gain weight, you might need a high-performance food. Personally, I have found that my Frenchies are very good at self-regulating their weight. None of mine are overweight or thin, and I let them adjust how much they want to eat on their own.

Feeding on a schedule helps your puppy get acclimated to life in your home and helps you judge when your puppy needs to go out.

Problem Eaters

On a rare occasion, you might run into a Frenchie that is a finicky eater. A dog will not starve himself . . . period. When he gets hungry, he will eat. Offer him food and, if he does not eat it, pick it up after fifteen minutes. Feed him again at his regular mealtimes. He will get hungry and eat again, and he will eat what you give him. Dogs are like children; sure, they'd rather eat junk food all day, but we must provide them with nutritious, balanced meals. Of course, if your dog is listless and refuses food, you should consult your veterinarian.

Treats

Treats are as much a part of your Frenchie's life as your own! Keep in mind that this is an approximately 20-pound (more or less) dog, and calories from treats should not make up more than 10 percent of his total caloric intake. A bit of cheese or chicken or a taste of pizza crust is fun for everybody, but do not get into the habit of feeding your dog from your plate. You will only create a begging monster. Do not give your Frenchie rich, spicy foods because intestinal disaster can occur. It is also important to make sure the bites you offer your Frenchie are Frenchie-size. In his eagerness to receive a treat, your dog may choke himself!

There are also many excellent dog treats available at your pet store. Once again, moderation is the key.

Even though treats are fun and are a wonderful incentive when it comes to training, it is best that about 90 percent of your Frenchie's calories come from his food, not from extra treats.

Supplements

If you are feeding a premium food, supplements are not really necessary. Ask your veterinarian for advice on this topic if you are in doubt.

Water

I cannot stress enough how important it is to have fresh water available to your Frenchie at all times. Check the water bowl several times a day or invest in one of the many watering devices that allows free-flowing water to be distributed into the bowls.

Change

Dogs do not get bored eating the same food every day. Their sense of smell is so great that they can detect a virtual cornucopia of smells with each whiff of their food bowl. It is also best to stay with the same manufacturer throughout the life of your Frenchie. He should go from puppy to adult to senior versions of the same brand of food. This will make for an easier transition to each life stage. Do not be tempted to switch foods for the sake of switching. If your Frenchie has a healthy, shiny coat, has bright eyes and is at a good weight, there is absolutely no need to switch foods.

chapter 6

Grooming
Your French
Bulldog

Even though she has a short, smooth coat, your Frenchie will require some basic maintenance to look and feel her best. Lucky you, you have chosen to share your life with one of the "wash 'n' wear" breeds. I have always respected and admired the work that goes into keeping Poodles and virtually all the terriers looking their best, but I do not want to be the one doing all that brushing, combing and clipping!

Get into the habit of "checking your Frenchie out" at least once a week, if not more often. Not only will you be able to perform routine grooming maintenance, you'll be able to catch some potential health problems before they escalate.

Coat Care

One of my personal favorite grooming tools is really just a glove. The Frenchies love it, and using it feels more like petting than grooming. There are several varieties made of several different materials. The one I use is like a glove with little rubber bumps on it. These nodules massage the skin and loosen and remove dead hair. My Joker will actually jump up and paw at my hands for me to hurry up and rub him when I put the glove on! These gloves are also available in sisal or horsehair. Use whatever pleases you and your Frenchie.

There is a wide variety of brushes to choose from when it comes to caring for your French Bulldog's coat. Use the kind you and your Frenchie both like best.

Of course, you can also use a soft-bristle dog brush or a curry comb-like brush. Slicker brushes (the wire ones) are not necessary for the Frenchie's close coat.

Ears

Those marvelous ears! They're so much a part of a Frenchie's personality and appeal, but they can also act as collection devices for every piece of dirt and grime imaginable. If your Frenchie shakes her head and carries it tilted to one side, she may have an ear infection. Do not delay—take her to the veterinarian. The veterinarian will culture the ear and determine the best course of treatment. Ear infections can be bacterial or yeast infections or several other types. The type of

61

treatment depends on the type of problem. Do not attempt to just clean the ears. Also, do not clean the ears prior to going to the veterinarian. He will need a good specimen of the problem. An untreated ear infection can lead to deafness, horrible growths inside the ear and an awful amount of discomfort for your beloved Frenchie.

For general ear cleaning, purchase a good canine ear cleaner from the pet store or from your veterinarian and use it as directed. Never use a cotton swab because the temptation is to dig down into the ear; use only a cotton ball and gently clean.

It is essential to clean your Frenchie's ears correctly to avoid nasty ear infections.

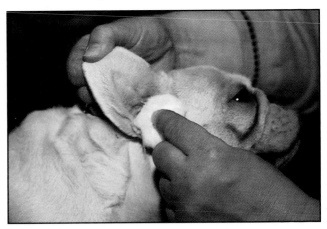

To clean and examine your Frenchie's ears, it is a good idea to make a habit of it from the time she is a puppy. Rub her tummy, get her relaxed and then gently squirt the ear cleaner into her ears. Gently massage the outside of the base of her ears to work the solution down into her ears. The other method is to squirt the cleaner onto a cotton ball and then swab her ear with it. This softens the dirt and wax that is in the ear. Do not push or poke down into the ear canal. This method can push dirt and debris into the ear and cause more problems than you may expect.

Next, use a different clean, solution-soaked cotton ball to gently swab the dirty solution and dirt out of her ear. She may never actually enjoy ear cleaning, but if you can make it tolerable, then it will not be such a chore.

Do not hesitate to consult your veterinarian if your Frenchie seems uncomfortable about ear cleaning. It could be a sign of an ear infection. There is some thought that allergies and other immune system problems can manifest themselves in chronic ear problems in French Bulldogs. Chronic, untreated ear infections can lead to requiring an operation that removes the entire ear canal, an expensive, painful and often very preventable surgery. Take ear problems very seriously—after all, those ears are one of the hallmarks of the breed!

Eyes

Those big chocolate eyes that melt your heart should be given special attention. There should not be excessive tearing or discharge. Frenchie eyes usually are relatively trouble-free, but be alert for any change in their appearance.

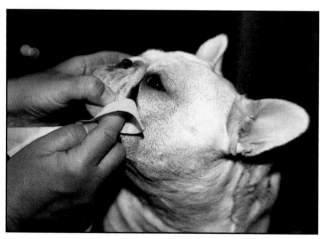

It is easy to keep the wrinkles around your Frenchie's nose clean with a baby wipe. Be gentle!

With just a little extra care, you can keep your Frenchie's eyes clean and problem-free. Once a week or so, maybe in conjunction with ear cleaning, get your Frenchie into a comfortable sitting position. Hold your hand so that you have control of her head. Gentle, yet firm is the key here; if you control or restrain too tightly, then she will probably resist. Using a moist cotton ball, gently clean around her eyes and take this opportunity to examine her eyes for any swelling, redness, blue tint to the eye, etc. Her eyes should be clear, bright and free of any abnormal amount of discharge. Unfortunately, lighter-colored Frenchies can also have some tear staining. This can be a good time to clean her face with a specially formulated tear-stain remover and keep her fresh and bright looking.

Teeth and Gums

Dogs do not get cavities like we do, but they can develop gum disease. Check for broken teeth and signs of inflammation or swelling at least once a week. Have your veterinarian check the teeth carefully during each annual exam. Plenty of dental chew toys can help prevent dental disease, but do not be surprised if your French Bulldog requires a professional dental cleaning on occasion.

Brushing your French Bulldog's teeth will reduce the risk of gum disease and will also make her annual tooth cleaning at the veterinarian's office less troublesome.

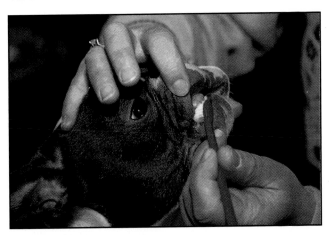

As you may know, there are wonderful doggie toothbrushes and toothpastes available for our Frenchies. Toothbrushes come in regular toothbrush-shaped types (but the bristles are *much* softer than even a child's toothbrush, so do not be tempted to use a human toothbrush), fingertip types that allow for a bit more control and even pads that are soaked in a tooth-cleaning solution to make doggie dental hygiene even easier. Once again, do not use human toothpaste, as it can upset your dog's stomach and the ingredients do not work properly for dogs. Canine toothpastes are specifically formulated for canine dental hygiene.

It may take a bit of time and patience for your Frenchie to become comfortable with the entire dental hygiene procedure. It's a good idea to give her some time to get used to the toothbrush. Play with her with it; let her bite it and mouth it before you actually brush her teeth with it. The taste of the toothpaste may also take a bit for her to become accustomed to, so don't rush her. Remember, this is something that you will be doing for her entire life—you want it to be pleasurable, or at the very least, tolerable for you both!

Dogs have more problems with broken teeth than you might expect, so do not hesitate to take her to the veterinarian if you see a broken tooth or any redness or swelling of her gums.

Nail trims should never be more than a month apart.

Toenails

This is probably the one area that is most uncomfortable for pet owners. It is critical to your Frenchie, however, to keep her nails short and stubby. If you get your puppy accustomed to having her feet handled and her nails clipped as a puppy, it will be easier as she matures. Our dogs cannot wear down their nails close enough naturally, but a daily walk on concrete can help keep them a little closer.

You can have your veterinarian, the breeder or a professional groomer show you how to trim your dog's nails. There are several types of nail trimmers available; use whatever is comfortable for you. Keep a bottle of styptic powder handy in case you cut a nail too close. Keep in mind that the nail does bleed, and yes, it does hurt, but it is more like when you clip a cuticle too closely, not cutting the toe itself! If you absolutely cannot bring yourself to cut your dog's nails or if you have a dog that puts up a struggle, do not stress yourself and your dog. Take her to a groomer or to your veterinarian twice a month or so (no less than once a month) and have him do it! It may well be worth it to all parties involved.

QUICK AND PAINLESS NAIL CLIPPING

This is possible if you make a habit of handling your dog's feet and giving your dog treats when you do. When it's time to clip nails, go through the same routine but take your clippers and snip off just the end of the nail. If you clip too far down, you'll cut into the "quick," or the nerve center, hurting your dog and causing the nail to bleed. Clip two nails a session while you're getting your dog used to the procedure. You'll soon be doing all four feet quickly and easily.

Various and Sundry Parts and Places

A little petroleum jelly, mineral oil or baby oil on your Frenchie's nose will keep the nose leather pliant and clean. Some Frenchies seem to develop a crusty film on their noses, and this will help eliminate that.

Your Frenchie's nose wrinkles may need extra attention. I recommend using a baby wipe–type towelette to clean the wrinkles every day or so. If your Frenchie has any irritation in these areas, apply some baby diaper-rash ointment into the creases. This is best done right before you go to bed, and it will be a bit messy the first few times you do it until you get the amount down pat.

Occasionally, a French Bulldog has an "inverted" tail. This means the tail is almost back up inside the body. It will be impossible for your Frenchie to keep this area clean on her own, so you must help her. Using the same type of baby-wipe towelette as you'd use on her face, gently wrap your finger with the towelette and clean around her tail. After cleaning, liberally apply more of the diaper-rash ointment around her tail area.

With their stocky bodies, Frenchies cannot twist and turn to attend to their personal hygiene. Once again, we must help them. If your Frenchie is female, ensure that her vulva is clean and free of discharge. If there is an unpleasant odor or discharge, consult your veterinarian. On your male Frenchie, check the inside of his back legs and the sheath of his penis for dirt or discharge; if present, clean him off. As always, if there is an odor or a discharge, consult your veterinarian.

Bathing Your Frenchie

Some Frenchies love taking a bath; others simply tolerate it. As in most things, if her first baths are painless and stress-free, she will enjoy them for the rest of her life. Use only a dog shampoo since dogs have a different pH level in their skin and coat than we do; human shampoo can damage their skin and coat.

Use a shampoo especially formulated for dogs to match the pH of your dog's skin and coat.

French Bulldogs should not be over-bathed; a weekly bath would probably be too often and could lead to a dull, dry, flaking coat. Of course, if your Frenchie gets dirty, she will need a bath! Sometimes what we might think is dirt is actually flaking from dry skin.

Select a gentle, tearless shampoo for her face and use whatever shampoo is appropriate for her coat on the rest of her. There are whitening shampoos for light-colored Frenchies, special shampoos to make dark Frenchies sparkle and an entire range of medicinal, moisturizing shampoos. Select whichever one best suits your Frenchie's needs.

If you have one, use the spray attachment in your sink or shower when bathing your Frenchie. The water should be warm but not too hot!

TOOLS FOR GROOMING YOUR FRENCH BULLDOG

pin brush

slicker brush

flea comb

towel

mat rake

grooming glove

scissors

nail clippers

tooth-cleaning equipment

shampoo

conditioner

clippers

I use the spray part of the shower head to saturate her with lukewarm water. Do not use hot water because it can dry her skin. Start with her face and work your way to her tail, making sure she is completely wet. Then wash her body with the shampoo formulated for her type and wash her face with the tearless shampoo. Rinse her off completely. If she is really dirty, repeat. When you think she is thoroughly rinsed off, rinse her again. Then allow her to shake the excess water off. This is part of being a dog. Towel her dry and praise her profusely. I always sing to my Frenchies or talk to them the entire time I am bathing them. My singing probably does not soothe anybody that might hear me, but the Frenchies seem to be distracted by it!

Do not bathe your Frenchie too frequently. Once a month, unless she gets dirty, is usually enough. Grooming time should be fun time. You are spending time with your Frenchie, and she is getting one-on-one attention. Enjoy having a squeaky clean, fresh-smelling Frenchie.

chapter 7

Keeping Your French Bulldog Healthy

French Bulldogs are an exaggerated breed with a unique set of challenges and the possibility of inherited conditions. Some of the very features that make them so adorable are features that can cause problems in their lives. The first step toward ensuring that your Frenchie leads a healthy life is to buy a healthy puppy from a reputable breeder. Your Frenchie should have healthy parents and healthy littermates.

Choosing a Veterinarian

This can be easier said than done. Many breeders will have waiting lists for certain colors and sexes and it can seem like an eternity when you want your Frenchie *now*! Just like your grandmother always told you, patience *is* a virtue and patience may very well be required as you wait for your Frenchie puppy. As we discussed in an earlier chapter, take your time and do your research.

Next, find a veterinarian that you trust and respect and that, hopefully, has experience with French Bulldogs. The flat faces of Bulldog breeds have their own unique set of needs when it comes to anesthesia and many procedures. Having a comfortable rapport with your veterinarian is essential. You must trust and respect your veterinarian. No matter how highly recommended a veterinarian is, if you do not enjoy your trips to see him, you need to select another one.

To find a veterinarian you trust, ask friends, neighbors and your breeder if you have one. The local kennel club may also be able to help.

Your veterinarian will be your partner in keeping your Frenchie healthy for many, many years. Take the time to choose wisely. Hopefully, your breeder will be able to recommend a veterinarian that he knows and trusts. If not, contact your area kennel club or just get out the Yellow Pages and start calling.

Make an appointment to have your new puppy checked within 72 hours of bringing him home. Your breeder may have a different requirement, but most will require that you have the dog checked as a precaution and to ensure that you have a veterinarian.

When you go in for the first visit, take all the information your breeder has provided—shot records, the health certificate and so on.

Vaccinations

Vaccine protocols may change as new data becomes available, so consult your veterinarian. She will help set up your new puppy with a complete schedule of vaccinations. Your puppy should be vaccinated in two-to four-week intervals until he is 12 to 20 weeks of age, depending on the vaccine used. The first shot should have been given by 6 to 7 weeks of age, and hopefully, your puppy will have two shots by the time you get him. A Rabies vaccination can be given after 12 weeks of age. All vaccines should be boostered at 1 year of age. Basic vaccinations should include Distemper, Parainfluenza, Parvovirus and Rabies. Vaccinations may or may not include Coronavirus, Bordetella (kennel cough), Lyme Disease and Leptospira (not used as frequently and associated with vaccination reactions).

YOUR PUPPY'S VACCINES

Vaccines are given to prevent your dog from getting infectious diseases like canine distemper or rabies. Vaccines are the ultimate preventive medicine: They're given before your dog ever gets the disease to protect him from the disease. That's why it is necessary for your dog to be vaccinated routinely. Puppy vaccines start by 8 weeks of age for the five-in-one DHLPP vaccine and are given every three to four weeks until the puppy is 16 months old. Your veterinarian will put your puppy on a proper schedule and will remind you when to bring in your dog for shots.

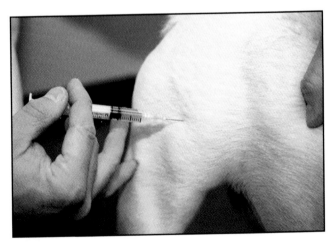

Your French Bulldog may have already had some of his shots when you bring him home. The veterinarian is the best source for information on vaccine protocol.

DISTEMPER

Distemper has been virtually eliminated, but it is still a nasty disease that affects the respiratory system, the neurological system and the gastrointestinal system.

Parvovirus and Coronavirus

Parvovirus and Coronavirus are viral diseases that are easily transmitted from one dog to another. These diseases can be carried on a person's shoes, hands, feet or clothing. Puppies and young dogs are the most easily affected, and once infected, nothing much can be done except to support the dog until the disease runs its course.

It is important to ensure that your Frenchie is flea-free, especially if he plays outside frequently.

Rabies

Rabies no longer is the threat it once was, but it still is very much a risk in certain parts of the country. Keep your Frenchie current on his rabies vaccination. It is required by law in every state, so there is absolutely no reason not to keep your dog current.

Bordetella

Bordetella, or kennel cough, is highly contagious, and your pet should be vaccinated for this disease if he will be exposed to other dogs frequently.

Lyme Disease

Lyme Disease is caused by ticks, and there is a vaccination that will prevent this deadly disease. Once again, check with your veterinarian to determine if Lyme Disease is a problem in your area.

Parasite Control

Your new puppy should have a stool sample checked for parasites as soon as possible; even if your puppy was given worming medication, no medication will work for all parasites. Repeat a stool sample parasite test two to four weeks after the first test to be sure your Frenchie is parasite-free. Most parasites have a life cycle of two to three weeks; therefore, it is possible to get a negative test initially and later find out that the puppy does have parasites.

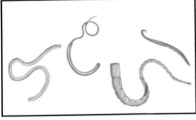

*Common inter-
nal parasites
(l-r): roundworm,
whipworm,
tapeworm and
hookworm.*

HOOKWORMS

Hookworms are a particularly nasty parasite. They attach to the intestinal wall and feed on tissue, causing inflammation, bleeding and even death if untreated. Treatment for hookworms may have to be repeated several times to eliminate the parasite.

ROUNDWORMS

Roundworms are very common in puppies and young dogs due to the ease with which they are transmitted. Roundworm eggs can even be passed from a mother to her puppies in utero. They are easily treated, so have your dog checked for roundworms.

WHIPWORMS

Whipworms are similar to roundworms but are very difficult to detect. They are also difficult to eradicate. Be patient and thorough in your worming, and you will get rid of them.

TAPEWORMS

Tapeworms are a relatively harmless worm, but it is very distressing to see the tiny little worm on your Frenchie's rear end. Tapeworms are visible to the naked eye and look like a piece of rice clinging to your dog's anal area. A regimen of tapeworm medicine will easily eradicate "tapes." This medicine is available by prescription only, so a trip to your veterinarian is necessary. Tapeworms come from ingesting flea eggs infected with tapeworms. If your dog is completely flea-free, he will probably be tapeworm-free.

HEARTWORM

Your veterinarian will recommend a schedule for a heartworm preventative, depending on the part of the country in which you live. Frenchies in Southern states will need year-round heartworm medication, but Frenchies in more northern climates will only need heartworm medication part of the year, during peak mosquito season.

A heartworm is a nasty parasite that lives in your dog's heart. Infestation is very preventable, so do not take any chances; give your Frenchie the appropriate preventative. Heartworm disease is transmitted by mosquitoes, so be especially careful if you live in mosquito-infested areas.

Heartworms pose a life-or-death threat to your Frenchie.

Your veterinarian should check your Frenchie's skin and coat for any parasites that might be there. Some are easily treatable; others can be debilitating such as generalized demodex mites.

FLEAS AND TICKS

Fleas

Fleas and ticks have plagued mankind (and dogkind) for eternity.

To rid your dog and home of fleas, you need to treat your dog *and* your home. Here's how:

- Identify where your pet(s) sleep. These are "hot spots."

- Clean your pet's bedding regularly by vacuuming and washing.

- Spray "hot spots" with a nontoxic, long-lasting flea larvicide.

- Treat outdoor "hot spots" with insecticide.

- Kill eggs on pets with a product containing insect growth regulators (IGRs).

- Kill fleas on pets per your veterinarian's recommendation.

It has only been in recent years that veterinary science has created a plethora of medicines and preventatives to enable us to provide virtually flea-free environments for our Frenchies.

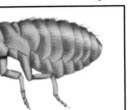

The flea is a die-hard pest.

There are so many safe, effective products available now to combat fleas and ticks that—thankfully—these pests are less of a problem. Prevention is key, however. Ask your veterinarian about starting your puppy on a flea/tick repellent right away. With this repellent, regular grooming and environmental controls, your dog and your home should stay pest-free. Without this attention, you risk infesting your dog and your home, and you're in for an ugly and costly battle to clear up the problem.

The first evidence of fleas may be your Frenchie's scratching. Fleas are fairly easy to see; they look like small, dark, moving specks. Flea bites cause local irritation, and common sites are the scrotum and under the tail, but bites can occur anywhere on your dog.

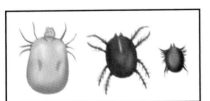

Three types of ticks (l-r): the wood tick, brown dog tick and deer tick.

Ticks

Ticks are hardy carriers of many diseases, including Rocky Mountain spotted fever, Lyme disease and encephalitis. A tick attaches itself to a dog by burying its head into the skin of the dog and sucking blood until the tick becomes bloated.

The best method for removing a tick is to grasp the tick as close to its head as possible with tweezers and a gloved hand and pull it straight out. First smear petroleum jelly or drop alcohol on the tick and let it sit for a minute. Grasp the tick with the tweezers and pull firmly to remove the entire head. If the head of the tick is left burrowed in the skin, it may lead to infection and possibly abscess. Swab the area with disinfectant and check the site for infection over the next few days. Consult with your veterinarian for the best course of action for your area.

Physical Examination

Your veterinarian should perform a complete physical examination. Ask about any inherited conditions that might affect his quality of life.

Your veterinarian should also discuss the proper care of your Frenchie's skin, ears and nails. Have your veterinarian show you the proper techniques to clean ears, facial wrinkles, and teeth and to trim nails.

Use tweezers to remove ticks from your dog.

Your Frenchie should have regular checkups throughout his life because some conditions do not appear until later in life.

Spaying and Neutering

As discussed in chapter 4, you should have your female Frenchie spayed before she comes into her first heat cycle to take advantage of the most health benefits. Having her spayed prior to her first heat cycle greatly reduces her chances of having mammary or uterine cancer. You will also be spared the mood swings, mess and inconvenience of heat cycles.

To lessen your male Frenchie's "leg lifting," it is recommended that he be neutered before he begins marking territory. Your veterinarian can provide more information on optimum times for neutering your dog. Neutering your male dog will have many benefits. He will be less aggressive toward other males, will have less desire to wander in search of females and will have a reduced risk of prostate cancer.

Your veterinarian will perform a complete physical examination on your Frenchie to make sure he is healthy and stays that way.

Run your hands regularly over your dog to feel for any injuries.

ADVANTAGES OF SPAYING OR NEUTERING YOUR FRENCH BULLDOG

Breeding French Bulldogs should not be undertaken lightly. Virtually all French Bulldogs are born by Cesarean section and bred by artificial insemination, so they are a difficult breed even for experienced breeders. This is a complicated breed with many factors about which even responsible, experienced breeders are still learning. The greatest advantage of spaying or neutering your Frenchie is eliminating the possibility of producing unwanted puppies. Other distinct advantages include:

No unwanted, messy heat cycles

A greatly decreased chance of pyometra (uterine infection) and breast cancer

No neighborhood dogs howling at your windows

Decreased incidence of prostate problems as he ages

Decreased aggressive behavior toward other males

Decreased tendency to wander (looking for love)

Decreased territorial marking

Conditions Found in French Bulldogs

The following conditions are thought to be inherited: deafness, stenotic nares (nostrils that are too small), dental and jaw malformations (wry jaw, missing/extra teeth), an elongated soft palate, a hypoplastic (collapsing) trachea, hernias (inguinal and umbilical), hip dysplasia, luxating patellas, skin disease (allergies/generalized demodex), heart murmurs/arrhythmias, vertebral anomalies (cannot be diagnosed without x-rays) and cryptorchidism (either or both testicles hidden).

Check your dog's teeth frequently and brush them regularly.

DEGENERATIVE DISC DISEASE

French Bulldogs can be prone to degenerative disc disease due to the dwarf body type. Unfortunately, this disease does not show up until the Frenchie is older, often 6 or 7 years of age. Your veterinarian should be on the lookout for this condition. French Bulldogs also have a tendency to have hemi-vertebrae, or malformed discs in the spine. Sometimes they can live their entire lives without experiencing any difficulties at all due to the "hemi's," or they may need to have surgery to alleviate the problems. These conditions are determined by taking x-rays of your Frenchie's spine.

HEMI-VERTEBRAE

Hemi-vertebrae are congenital malformations of the spine and are also seen in screw-tailed type dogs like

Boston Terriers and Bulldogs. This means they are present at birth. Hemi-vertebrae are formed when the two sides of the spine part do not properly fuse or connect. This causes a butterfly or wedge-shaped appearance when viewed on an x-ray from above. This can cause compression on the spine as the Frenchie matures. Any compression on the spine can cause problems. This may manifest itself in paralysis (complete or partial), weakness in the legs or discomfort (of various degrees). Many French Bulldogs can lead full, complete and pain-free lives with hemi-vertebrae, but obviously it is not a desirable condition and any spinal malformation is a warning flag.

*Frenchies, like
all purebred
dogs, tend to
have breed-
specific health
concerns of
which you
and your
veterinarian
should be aware.*

Most hemi-vertebrae seem to be in the thoracic area (neck) and this area seems to be the place to have a "hemi," if there are any at all. Unfortunately, hemi-vertebrae are very common in Frenchies and seem to almost be "part" of the breed. This does *not* mean that hemi-vertebrae are to be condoned or approved of, just that we need to be realistic about their occurrence.

Most reputable breeders x-ray their French Bulldogs that are to be used for breeding. X-raying them does not guarantee that there will be no hemi-vertebrae, it just means that the breeder then has more knowledge with which to make realistic and educated choices in their breeding program. If a breeder tells you that they have never had *any* hemi-vertebrae in their dogs, then they have probably not looked!

Most spinal problems that occur in French Bulldogs are caused by degenerative disc disease. This is a frustrating and devastating problem for breeders. Most French Bulldogs do not show any sign of degenerative disc disease until they are older and by then, they might have been used extensively in a breeding program. The breeder has done nothing wrong, but the damage is done. Degenerative disc disease is when the disc that cushions the spine degenerates or deteriorates into a less elastic, "dried out" cushion. This in itself does not cause problems, but when the disc is pushed into the spinal canal, it can cause swelling, pain and may even push the entire disc out of place. Veterinarians have many different names for this: herniated discs, protruding discs, ruptured discs and more.

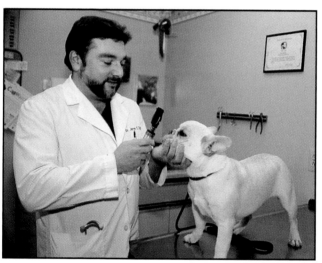

If you are ever in doubt when it comes to your French Bulldog's health, consult your veterinarian.

The first signs of degenerative disc disease may occur as early as three to five years. The younger the dog is when the problem surfaces, the less optimistic the outcome.

The first signs may be your Frenchie walking with her head held at an unnatural angle. She will appear to be in discomfort and may even yelp in pain when you pick

81

her up. She may trip and stumble a bit as she walks. This is not a time to be slow to call the vet—your Frenchie is in pain and needs help immediately!

More severe cases may lead to partial or complete paralysis of the rear legs. If you discover your French Bulldog unable to stand, immediately take her to the veterinarian. Put her in her crate so that she is stable and secure and go!

Your veterinarian may give her an injection (usually some type of steroids) to reduce the swelling and allow her to regain mobility. This may be followed by oral medications and crate rest. The crate rest may well be one of the most important parts of the treatment. Follow your veterinarians advice and do not be tempted to stop the crate confinement too early.

Surgery may be required, in which case you may wish to obtain a second opinion. There is a variety of surgical techniques to help alleviate the condition. Once again, if this were to become necessary for your Frenchie, your veterinarians would be able to discuss all options with you.

BREATHING PROBLEMS

In addition, breathing problems (elongated soft palettes, stenotic nares) can occur. Having an elongated soft palette is somewhat like having enlarged tonsils or extra tissue in the throat area. When a Frenchie with an elongated soft palette gets overheated, this tissue swells, can restrict his breathing and can even lead to death in very extreme cases. Surgical procedures can correct this problem, but it is a difficult surgery with an intense postoperative recovery period.

A sign that your Frenchie may have an elongated soft palette is if she frequently gags and brings up a foamy, fluffy phlegm, with no food. Her breathing may also be labored and very loud. This condition can be deadly in hotter, more humid parts of the country. As endearing as Frenchie snorts, snuffles and rattles may be, they can be a warning sign that there is a breathing problem.

Stenotic nares occur when the nostrils are very pinched in, restricting the Frenchie's ability to breathe freely and easily. If a Frenchie is breathing a lot harder than the normal Frenchie snuffling and gentle snorting, one of the above conditions may be involved. Your veterinarian will be better able to answer questions about these conditions. You should directly ask the breeder if either parent has had surgery for any of these conditions. To definitively diagnose these conditions, your Frenchie will have to be examined under general anesthesia.

LUXATING PATELLA

Luxating patellas (slipping kneecaps) are a common condition in French Bulldogs. It is thought that as many as 50 percent of all French Bulldogs have some degree of luxating patellas. Some Frenchies can live with some degree of luxation their entire life with no discomfort or trouble; others must have a surgical procedure to lead a comfortable life. Fortunately, this surgery is a one-time event, and your Frenchie can then go on to lead a normal life. This condition is determined by either manual palpation by an experienced veterinarian or by x-rays.

HIP DYSPLASIA

Hip dysplasia is occasionally found in Frenchies. This condition occurs when the hip joint does not fit as deeply into the socket as it should. Since they are smaller dogs, this condition may or may not affect a French Bulldog's quality of life. Some Frenchies may be more bothered by hip dysplasia and require surgery to have a comfortable life. Others may not be bothered at all. Not allowing your Frenchie to become overweight can be helpful if he has some degree of hip dysplasia. This condition is determined by taking x-rays of your Frenchie's hips.

ALLERGIES

Allergies are common in French Bulldogs. The bulk of allergies are topical, or caused by something in the environment. Grass, dust, pollen and smoke all can be allergens to your Frenchie. Only a canine dermatologist can determine exactly what your Frenchie is allergic to. Allergies can often manifest themselves in excessive licking or chewing of the feet. Few true food allergies exist in dogs. Check with your veterinarian if your Frenchie seems to have symptoms of allergies.

Your French Bulldog may have allergic reactions toward something in his environment, whether inside or out.

Allergies can be a frustrating condition to diagnose and to then deal with. Your veterinarian may suggest a variety of tests be run on your French Bulldog and it will be well worth the expense and effort. Your Frenchie cannot understand what is wrong; she just knows that she itches and then she chews at herself to relieve it! There is some thought that French Bulldogs may not, as a rule, have the most effective immune systems and this may manifest itself in allergies. In fact, it may be an overly reactive immune systems that causes the Frenchie's body to attack normally benign substances. Allergies to many things in the environment can be causing your Frenchie to itch. The constant chewing and sucking may then cause infections that lead to an entire new set of problems. Allergies can threaten the quality of your French Bulldogs life dramatically. Please, consult your veterinarian as to the best course of action.

Many French Bulldogs are sensitive to bee stings, etc. just like some people may be. It is a good idea to have a liquid antihistamine on hand, just in case.

Misshapen Jaw

Occasionally, a Frenchie may have a "wry" or misshapen jaw. This usually does not cause any discomfort to the Frenchie, but the tongue may protrude, keeping him from a career as a show dog.

These are some of the most common inherited conditions seen in French Bulldogs. Your veterinarian can determine the presence and severity of these conditions.

Giving Medicines

Medications should *never* be given without the recommendation of your veterinarian. Always give all of the prescription; do not be tempted to stop because your French Bulldog seems to be doing better.

Pills and Capsules

It can be as easy to give a pill as you make it. Some Frenchies are tricked by hiding the pill in a bit of cheese, peanut butter or, my favorite, cream cheese. Quickly open your dog's mouth and push the pill as far back in his throat as you can, gently holding his mouth shut until he swallows. Praise and reassure your Frenchie throughout this entire procedure. The key is to do it quickly and not let giving a little pill become a battle of wills.

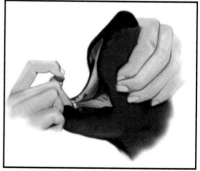

To give a pill, open the mouth wide, then drop it in the back of the throat.

85

LIQUID MEDICINE

Liquid medicines are much easier to give. Simply pull up the prescribed liquid into a plastic syringe (without a needle) and smoothly squirt the medicine into the side of the dog's mouth in between his lip and back

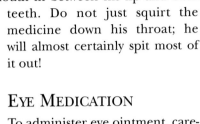

teeth. Do not just squirt the medicine down his throat; he will almost certainly spit most of it out!

EYE MEDICATION

To administer eye ointment, carefully pull down your Frenchie's eyelid, creating a pocket in which to drop the medication. If you

Squeeze eye ointment into the lower lid.

have any doubts about the directions for administering medication, call your veterinarian.

Taking Temperature

A healthy puppy has bright eyes and a muscular body and while he is awake will be playful and happy. Should he show signs of lethargy or weakness and you don't know the cause, telephone your vet and take him in for a checkup. As a preliminary step you can take his temperature so that you will know if he has a fever. Use a rectal thermometer lubricated with petroleum jelly and insert it about three-fourths of an inch into the rectum. Normal temperature is about 101°F, give or take a degree. It is better to err on the side of caution with a puppy and be ready to take him to the vet at any sign of a fever.

Simple First Aid

I cannot stress enough how important it is not to delay in the event of an emergency and to get your beloved Frenchie to your veterinarian (or an emergency veterinarian) as soon as possible. Now is not the time to scrimp! Below are a few tips that may help you stabilize your Frenchie until you can get him to your

veterinarian.

BEE OR OTHER INSECT STINGS

French Bulldogs can be prone to insect bite reactions. With their smaller tracheas, it can be critical that you react quickly if your Frenchie is stung. At your first veterinarian visit, ask for the appropriate dosage of Benadryl™ for your Frenchie and always have it on hand. I use the liquid type; it is absorbed more quickly. Your Frenchie may have hives or a swollen face if he gets stung. Give the appropriate amount of Benadryl™. If in any doubt in the event of a sting, call your veterinarian.

ANIMAL BITES

If your Frenchie is bitten by another dog or another domestic animal, find out the status of the attacker's rabies vaccinations. Hopefully, your Frenchie is current on his rabies shots. If the wound is not severe, clean it thoroughly and call your veterinarian. If it's severe, do not delay—get to your veterinarian. One problem with puncture bites is that they may not look bad, but they can become infected very easily.

BLEEDING

If there is a wound, apply pressure using a clean cloth or ice pack. Determine if the amount of blood requires an immediate trip to the veterinarian.

An Elizabethan collar keeps your dog from licking a fresh wound.

Any vomiting of blood or rectal or vaginal bleeding (your pet bitch will have been spayed so no heat cycles for her!) requires veterinarian care and diagnosis.

VOMITING

If your dog vomits one time, it is probably nothing to be overly concerned about. If it is continual or there is blood, garbage or an unidentifiable substance in the vomit, it is best to consult your veterinarian.

DIARRHEA

As with vomiting, if it is a one-time episode or lasts only a day, it is probably not a major concern. But if your Frenchie has blood in the stool, if the diarrhea lasts for more than 24 hours, or if there seems to be undigested food in the stool, a trip to the veterinarian is probably warranted. If possible, collect a sample of the diarrhea in a plastic sandwich bag for your veterinarian to examine.

HEAT STROKE

As previously discussed, French Bulldogs do *not* tolerate heat and humidity well at all. If your Frenchie appears disoriented, is panting wildly and has a wild look in his eyes when it is hot, he may be overheating. Put him under cool, not cold, running water. Concentrate on cooling him off in the groin area on his underside. If he seems to cool down relatively quickly, you are probably out of danger. If in doubt, do not hesitate to call your veterinarian.

Take his temperature; if it is over 103°, call your veterinarian immediately. Continue to take his temperature until it is normal (in the 101° range). Your Frenchie may have some stomach upset for the next few hours, caused by the shock to his system. Allow him access to cool water and feed only half rations for his evening meal.

If you do not have access to cool, running water, use ice packs. My car's air-conditioning system once broke on the way home from a dog show on a hot summer day. I stopped at the next store, bought two bags of ice and several bottles of water. I opened the bags of ice into the dogs' crates and literally had my Frenchies "on ice." All the way home, I stopped periodically to saturate the dogs completely and

---

POISON ALERT

If your dog has ingested a potentially poisonous substance, waste no time. Call the National Animal Poison Control Center hot line:

1-800-548-2423 ($30 per case)

or

1-900-680-0000 ($20 for the first five minutes, $2.95 for each additional minute)

---

refresh their water bowls. Thanks to all of these precautions, we made it home fine.

POISONING

Prevention is the best plan of attack for poison control. Do not ever leave anything at Frenchie level that could make him sick. There is such an enormous range of remedies and different actions to take in the event of poisoning that I hesitate to recommend any general courses of action. Have the telephone number for a poison-control center available and be ready to read them the entire label. The trained professionals will be able to best advise you what to do.

Some of the many household substances harmful to your dog.

BROKEN BONES

This is no time for delay. Support the broken bone as best you can and immediately go to your veterinarian. You might wrap a rolled-up newspaper around the leg and tape it into place or put the leg on a pillow and tape it gently to the pillow.

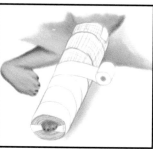

Make a temporary splint by wrapping the leg in firm casing, then bandaging it.

CHOKING

If your Frenchie appears to be choking, reach in his mouth and try to pull out whatever may be choking him. Clear an airway by pulling his tongue out. If your Frenchie continues to try to vomit, he must go to the veterinarian for treatment.

ITEMS FOR YOUR FRENCHIE MEDICINE CABINET

Keep a canine first-aid kit on hand for general care and emergencies. Check it periodically to make sure liquids haven't spilled or dried up, and replace medications and materials after they're used. Your kit should include:

Benadryl™

Kaopectate™

Pepto Bismol™

Hydrogen peroxide (as a cleanser)

A thermometer (rectal)

Elastic bandages

Gauze

Petroleum jelly

Baby oil

Cotton balls

A plastic syringe

Tweezers

Dog aspirin (not ibuprofen)

Antibacterial ointment

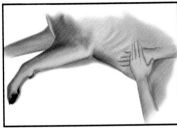

Applying abdominal thrusts can save a choking dog.

Transporting Your Injured Frenchie

If your Frenchie has an episode where he "goes down" or becomes paralyzed in his legs or back, time is of the essence. Immediately take him to the veterinarian, who will determine a course of action. Put him in a crate and carefully drive to the veterinarian.

The best way to transport an injured Frenchie to the veterinarian will almost always be in his crate. If possible, have someone go with you so you can watch him during the trip.

Identifying Your Dog

It's a terrible thing to think about, but your dog could somehow, someday, get lost or stolen. How would you get him back? Your best bet would be to have some form of identification on your dog. You can choose from a collar and tags, a tattoo, a microchip or a combination of these three.

Every dog should wear a buckle collar with identification tags. They are the quickest and easiest way for a stranger to identify your dog. It's best to inscribe the tags with your name and phone number; you don't need to include your dog's name.

As your Frenchie ages, he may not have as much energy as he once did. Make sure you soften his food if he has trouble with hard kibble and be patient if he is not perfect with housetraining anymore. Lots of love is what he needs most.

There are two ways to permanently identify your dog. The first is a tattoo, placed on the inside of your dog's thigh. The tattoo should be your social security number or your dog's American Kennel Club registration number.

The second method is a microchip, a rice-sized pellet that's inserted under the dog's skin at the base of the neck, between the shoulder blades. When a scanner is passed over the dog, it will beep, notifying the person running the scanner that the dog has a microchip. The scanner will then read a code which identifies the dog. Microchips are becoming more and more popular and are certainly the wave of the future.

The Geriatric French Bulldog

The day will come when Father Time begins to catch up with your Frenchie. He may begin to gray in his muzzle; he may sleep more or be a little quicker to tire when playing or on his walks. Be aware of this and adjust his activity level accordingly. Respect the aged Frenchie; he is to be treasured. Feed him a premium food developed for senior dogs and soften his food if he seems to have trouble eating the hard kibble.

Be patient with him if he is not as reliable as he once was in his housetraining. He has given you his entire life; he deserves the best of care in his golden years.

When to Go to Your Veterinarian

I always err on the side of caution. I would rather make the occasional extra trip to the veterinarian than berate myself with, "If I had only gone to the veterinarian . . . "

Try to gather as much information as possible when you go to the veterinarian. When did you first see the behavior? How long has he been having diarrhea? Have answers to any questions that may help the veterinarian make an accurate diagnosis.

Emergencies include:

- acute abdominal pain
- suspected poisoning
- snakebite
- burns
- frostbite
- shock
- dehydration
- abnormal bleeding
- violent diarrhea or vomiting
- deep wounds

You are the best judge of your dog's health, as you live with and observe him every day. Don't hesitate to call your veterinarian if you suspect trouble.

The Final Goodbye

There may come a time when the quality of your dog's life is gone and he no longer enjoys life as he used to. This may be the time for one of life's hardest decisions. Talk to your veterinarian and determine what is best for your dear companion and you and your family. Everyone deals with this in a different manner. I feel the greatest gift I can give my dogs is for them to pass on knowing that they are loved and secure and that their lives were important to me.

Your Happy, Healthy Pet

Your Dog's Name _____

Name on Your Dog's Pedigree (if your dog has one) _____

_____

Where Your Dog Came From _____

_____

Your Dog's Birthday _____

Your Dog's Veterinarian

    Name _____

    Address _____

    Phone Number_____

    Emergency Number_____

Your Dog's Health

    Vaccines

    type _____ date given _____

    type _____ date given _____

    type _____ date given _____

    type _____ date given _____

    Heartworm

    date tested _____ type used_____ start date _____

Your Dog's License Number_____

Groomer's Name and Number _____

Dogsitter/Walker's Name and Number_____

Awards Your Dog Has Won

    Award _____ date earned _____

    Award _____ date earned _____

part three

Enjoying
your
Dog

chapter 8

Basic
Training

by Ian Dunbar, Ph.D., MRCVS

Training is the jewel in the crown—the most important aspect of doggy husbandry. There is no more important variable influencing dog behavior and temperament than the dog's education: A well-trained, well-behaved and good-natured puppydog is always a joy to live with, but an untrained and un-civilized dog can be a perpetual nightmare. Moreover, deny the dog an education and she will not have the opportunity to fulfill her own canine potential; neither will she have the ability to communicate effectively with her human companions.

Luckily, modern psychological training methods are easy, efficient, effective and, above all, considerably dog-friendly and user-friendly.

Doggy education is as simple as it is enjoyable. But before you can have a good time play-training with your new dog, you have to learn what to do and how to do it. There is no bigger variable influencing the success of dog training than the *owner's* experience and expertise. *Before you embark on the dog's education, you must first educate yourself.*

Basic Training for Owners

Ideally, basic owner training should begin well *before* you select your dog. Find out all you can about your chosen breed first, then master rudimentary training and handling skills. If you already have your puppy-dog, owner training is a dire emergency—the clock is ticking! Especially for puppies, the first few weeks at home are the most important and influential days in the dog's life. Indeed, the cause of most adolescent and adult problems may be traced back to the initial days the pup explores her new home. This is the time to establish the *status quo*—to teach the puppydog how you would like her to behave and so prevent otherwise quite predictable problems.

In addition to consulting breeders and breed books such as this one (which understandably have a positive breed bias), seek out as many pet owners with your breed as you can find. Good points are obvious. What you want to find out are the breed-specific *problems*, so you can nip them in the bud. In particular, you should talk to owners with *adolescent* dogs and make a list of all anticipated problems. Most important, *test drive* at least half a dozen adolescent and adult dogs of your breed yourself. An 8-week-old puppy is deceptively easy to handle, but she will acquire adult size, speed and strength in just four months, so you should learn now what to prepare for.

Puppy and pet dog training classes offer a convenient venue to locate pet owners and observe dogs in action. For a list of suitable trainers in your area, contact the Association of Pet Dog Trainers (see chapter 13). You may also begin your basic owner training by observing other owners in class. Watch as many classes and test drive as many dogs as possible. Select an upbeat, dog-friendly, people-friendly, fun-and-games, puppydog pet training class to learn the ropes. Also, watch training videos and read training books. You must find out what to do and how to do it *before* you have to do it.

Principles of Training

Most people think training comprises teaching the dog to do things such as sit, speak and roll over, but even a 4-week-old pup knows how to do these things already. Instead, the first step in training involves teaching the dog human words for each dog behavior and activity and for each aspect of the dog's environment. That way you, the owner, can more easily participate in the dog's domestic education by directing her to perform specific actions appropriately, that is, at the right time, in the right place and so on. Training opens communication channels, enabling an educated dog to at least understand her owner's requests.

In addition to teaching a dog *what* we want her to do, it is also necessary to teach her *why* she should do what we ask. Indeed, 95 percent of training revolves around motivating the dog *to want to do* what we want. Dogs often understand what their owners want; they just don't see the point of doing it—especially when the owner's repetitively boring and seemingly senseless instructions are totally at odds with much more pressing and exciting doggy distractions. It is not so much the dog that is being stubborn or dominant; rather, it is the owner who has failed to acknowledge the dog's needs and feelings and to approach training from the dog's point of view.

THE MEANING OF INSTRUCTIONS

The secret to successful training is learning how to use training lures to predict or prompt specific behaviors—to coax the dog to do what you want *when* you want. Any highly valued object (such as a treat or toy) may be used as a lure, which the dog will follow with her eyes and nose. Moving the lure in specific ways entices the dog to move her nose, head and entire body in specific ways. In fact, by learning the art of manipulating various lures, it is possible to teach the dog to assume virtually any body position and perform any action. Once you have control over the expression of the dog's behaviors and can elicit any body position or behavior at will, you can easily teach the dog to perform on request.

Teach your dog words for each activity she needs to know, like down.

Tell your dog what you want her to do, use a lure to entice her to respond correctly, then profusely praise and maybe reward her once she performs the desired action. For example, verbally request "Tina, sit!" while you move a squeaky toy upwards and backwards over the dog's muzzle (lure-movement and hand signal), smile knowingly as she looks up (to follow the lure) and sits down (as a result of canine anatomical engineering), then praise her to distraction ("Gooood Tina!"). Squeak the toy, offer a training treat and give your dog and yourself a pat on the back.

Being able to elicit desired responses over and over enables the owner to reward the dog over and over. Consequently, the dog begins to think training is fun. For example, the more the dog is rewarded for sitting, the more she enjoys sitting. Eventually the dog comes

101

to realize that, whereas most sitting is appreciated, sitting immediately upon request usually prompts especially enthusiastic praise and a slew of high-level rewards. The dog begins to sit on cue much of the time, showing that she is starting to grasp the meaning of the owner's verbal request and hand signal.

WHY COMPLY?

Most dogs enjoy initial lure-reward training and are only too happy to comply with their owners' wishes. Unfortunately, repetitive drilling without appreciative feedback tends to diminish the dog's enthusiasm until she eventually fails to see the point of complying anymore. Moreover, as the dog approaches adolescence she becomes more easily distracted as she develops other interests. Lengthy sessions with repetitive exercises tend to bore and demotivate both parties. If it's not fun, the owner doesn't do it and neither does the dog.

Integrate training into your dog's life: The greater number of training sessions each day and the *shorter* they are, the more willingly compliant your dog will

To train your dog, you need gentle hands, a loving heart and a good attitude.

become. Make sure to have a short (just a few seconds) training interlude before every enjoyable canine activity. For example, ask your dog to sit to greet people, to sit before you throw her Frisbee and to sit for her supper. Really, sitting is no different from a canine "Please." Also, include numerous short training interludes during every enjoyable canine pastime, for example, when playing with the dog or when she is running in the park. In this fashion, doggy distractions may be effectively converted into rewards for training. Just as all games have rules, fun becomes training . . . and training becomes fun.

Eventually, rewards actually become unnecessary to continue motivating your dog. If trained with consideration and kindness, performing the desired behaviors will become self-rewarding and, in a sense, your dog will motivate herself. Just as it is not necessary to reward a human companion during an enjoyable walk in the park, or following a game of tennis, it is hardly necessary to reward our best friend—the dog—for walking by our side or while playing fetch. Human company during enjoyable activities is reward enough for most dogs.

Even though your dog has become self-motivating, it's still good to praise and pet her a lot and offer rewards once in a while, especially for a good job well done. And if for no other reason, praising and rewarding others is good for the human heart.

Punishment

Without a doubt, lure-reward training is by far the best way to teach: Entice your dog to do what you want and then reward her for doing so. Unfortunately, a human shortcoming is to take the good for granted and to moan and groan at the bad. Specifically, the dog's many good behaviors are ignored while the owner focuses on punishing the dog for making mistakes. In extreme cases, instruction is *limited* to punishing mistakes made by a trainee dog, child, employee or husband, even though it has been proven punishment training is notoriously inefficient and ineffective and is decidedly unfriendly and combative. It teaches the dog that training is a drag, almost as quickly as it teaches the dog to dislike her trainer. Why treat our best friends like our worst enemies?

Punishment training is also much more laborious and time consuming. Whereas it takes only a finite amount of time to teach a dog what to chew, for example, it takes much, much longer to punish the dog for each and every mistake. Remember, *there is only one right way!* So why not teach that right way from the outset?!

To make matters worse, punishment training causes severe lapses in the dog's reliability. Since it is obviously impossible to punish the dog each and every time she misbehaves, the dog quickly learns to distinguish between those times when she must comply (so as to avoid impending punishment) and those times when she need not comply, because punishment is impossible. Such times include when the dog is off leash and 6 feet away, when the owner is otherwise engaged (talking to a friend, watching television, taking a shower, tending to the baby or chatting on the telephone) or when the dog is left at home alone.

Instances of misbehavior will be numerous when the owner is away, because even when the dog complied in the owner's looming presence, she did so unwillingly. The dog was forced to act against her will, rather than molding her will to want to please. Hence, when the owner is absent, not only does the dog know she need not comply, she simply does not want to. Again, the trainee is not a stubborn vindictive beast, but rather the trainer has failed to teach. Punishment training invariably creates unpredictable Jekyll and Hyde behavior.

Trainer's Tools

Many training books extol the virtues of a vast array of training paraphernalia and electronic and metallic gizmos, most of which are designed for canine restraint, correction and punishment, rather than for actual facilitation of doggy education. In reality, most effective training tools are not found in stores; they come from within ourselves. In addition to a willing dog, all you really need is a functional human brain, gentle hands, a loving heart and a good attitude.

In terms of equipment, all dogs do require a quality buckle collar to sport dog tags and to attach the leash (for safety and to comply with local leash laws). Hollow chew toys (like Kongs or sterilized longbones) and a dog bed or collapsible crate are musts for housetraining. Three additional tools are required:

1. specific lures (training treats and toys) to predict and prompt specific desired behaviors;

2. rewards (praise, affection, training treats and toys) to reinforce for the dog what a lot of fun it all is; and

3. knowledge—how to convert the dog's favorite activities and games (potential distractions to training) into "life-rewards," which may be employed to facilitate training.

The most powerful of these is *knowledge*. Education is the key! Watch training classes, participate in training classes, watch videos, read books, enjoy play-training with your dog and then your dog will say "Please," and your dog will say "Thank you!"

Housetraining

If dogs were left to their own devices, certainly they would chew, dig and bark for entertainment and then no doubt highlight a few areas of their living space with sprinkles of urine, in much the same way we decorate by hanging pictures. Consequently, when we ask a dog to live with us, we must teach her *where* she may dig, *where* she may perform her toilet duties, *what* she may chew and *when* she may bark. After all, when left at home alone for many hours, we cannot expect the dog to amuse herself by completing crosswords or watching the soaps on TV!

Also, it would be decidedly unfair to keep the house rules a secret from the dog, and then get angry and punish the poor critter for inevitably transgressing rules she did not even know existed. Remember: Without adequate education and guidance, the dog will be forced to establish her own rules—doggy rules—and most probably will be at odds with the owner's view of domestic living.

Since most problems develop during the first few days the dog is at home, prospective dog owners must be certain they are quite clear about the principles of housetraining *before* they get a dog. Early misbehaviors quickly become established as the *status quo*—

becoming firmly entrenched as hard-to-break bad habits, which set the precedent for years to come. Make sure to teach your dog good habits right from the start. Good habits are just as hard to break as bad ones!

Ideally, when a new dog comes home, try to arrange for someone to be present as much as possible during the first few days (for adult dogs) or weeks for puppies. With only a little forethought, it is surprisingly easy to find a puppy sitter, such as a retired person, who would be willing to eat from your refrigerator and watch your television while keeping an eye on the newcomer to encourage the dog to play with chew toys and to ensure she goes outside on a regular basis.

POTTY TRAINING

To teach the dog where to relieve herself:

1. never let her make a single mistake;
2. let her know where you want her to go; and
3. handsomely reward her for doing so: "GOOOOOOOD DOG!!!" liver treat, liver treat, liver treat!

Preventing Mistakes

A single mistake is a training disaster, since it heralds many more in future weeks. And each time the dog soils the house, this further reinforces the dog's unfortunate preference for an indoor, carpeted toilet. *Do not let an unhousetrained dog have full run of the house.*

When you are away from home, or cannot pay full attention, confine the dog to an area where elimination is appropriate, such as an outdoor run or, better still, a small, comfortable indoor kennel with access to an outdoor run. When confined in this manner, most dogs will naturally housetrain themselves.

If that's not possible, confine the dog to an area, such as a utility room, kitchen, basement or garage, where elimination may not be desired in the long run but as an interim measure it is certainly preferable to doing it all around the house. Use newspaper to cover the floor of the dog's day room. The newspaper may be used to soak up the urine and to wrap up and dispose of the feces. Once your dog develops a preferred spot for eliminating, it is only necessary to cover that part of the floor with newspaper. The smaller papered area may then be moved (only a little each day) towards the door to the outside. Thus the dog will develop the tendency to go to the door when she needs to relieve herself.

Never confine an unhousetrained dog to a crate for long periods. Doing so would force the dog to soil the crate and ruin its usefulness as an aid for housetraining (see the following discussion).

Teaching Where

In order to teach your dog where you would like her to do her business, you have to be there to direct the proceedings—an obvious, yet often neglected, fact of life. In order to be there to teach the dog *where* to go, you need to know *when* she needs to go. Indeed, the success of housetraining depends on the owner's ability to predict these times. Certainly, a regular feeding schedule will facilitate prediction somewhat, but there is nothing like "loading the deck" and influencing the timing of the outcome yourself!

Whenever you are at home, make sure the dog is under constant supervision and/or confined to a small

The first few weeks at home are the most important and influential in your dog's life.

area. If already well trained, simply instruct the dog to lie down in her bed or basket. Alternatively, confine the dog to a crate (doggy den) or tie-down (a short, 18-inch lead that can be clipped to an eye hook in the baseboard near her bed). Short-term close confinement strongly inhibits urination and defecation, since the dog does not want to soil her sleeping area. Thus, when you release the puppydog each hour, she will definitely need to urinate immediately and defecate every third or fourth hour. Keep the dog confined to her doggy den and take her to her intended toilet area each hour, every hour and on the hour.

When taking your dog outside, instruct her to sit quietly before opening the door—she will soon learn to sit by the door when she needs to go out!

Teaching Why

Being able to predict when the dog needs to go enables the owner to be on the spot to praise and reward the dog. Each hour, hurry the dog to the intended toilet area in the yard, issue the appropriate instruction ("Go pee!" or "Go poop!"), then give the dog three to four minutes to produce. Praise and offer a couple of training treats when successful. The treats are important because many people fail to praise their dogs with feeling . . . and housetraining is hardly the time for understatement. So either loosen up and enthusiastically praise that dog: "Wuzzzer-wuzzer-wuzzer, hoooser good wuffer den? Hoooo went pee for Daddy?" Or say "Good dog!" as best you can and offer the treats for effect.

Following elimination is an ideal time for a spot of play-training in the yard or house. Also, an empty dog may be allowed greater freedom around the house for the next half hour or so, just as long as you keep an eye out to make sure she does not get into other kinds of mischief. If you are preoccupied and cannot pay full attention, confine the dog to her doggy den once more to enjoy a peaceful snooze or to play with her many chew toys.

If your dog does not eliminate within the allotted time outside—no biggie! Back to her doggy den, and then try again after another hour.

As I own large dogs, I always feel more relaxed walking an empty dog, knowing that I will not need to finish our stroll weighted down with bags of feces!

Beware of falling into the trap of walking the dog to get her to eliminate. The good ol' dog walk is such an enormous highlight in the dog's life that it represents the single biggest potential reward in domestic dogdom. However, when in a hurry, or during inclement weather, many owners abruptly terminate the walk the moment the dog has done her business. This, in effect, severely punishes the dog for doing the right thing, in the right place at the right time. Consequently, many dogs become strongly inhibited from eliminating outdoors because they know it will signal an abrupt end to an otherwise thoroughly enjoyable walk.

Instead, instruct the dog to relieve herself in the yard prior to going for a walk. If you follow the above instructions, most dogs soon learn to eliminate on cue. As soon as the dog eliminates, praise (and offer a treat or two)—"Good dog! Let's go walkies!" Use the walk as a reward for eliminating in the yard. If the dog does not go, put her back in her doggy den and think about a walk later on. You will find with a "No feces—no walk" policy, your dog will become one of the fastest defecators in the business.

If you do not have a backyard, instruct the dog to eliminate right outside your front door prior to the walk. Not only will this facilitate clean up and disposal of the feces in your own trash can but, also, the walk may again be used as a colossal reward.

CHEWING AND BARKING

Short-term close confinement also teaches the dog that occasional quiet moments are a reality of domestic living. Your puppydog is extremely impressionable during her first few weeks at home. Regular confinement at this time soon exerts a calming influence over the dog's personality. Remember, once the dog is housetrained and calmer, there will be a whole lifetime ahead for the dog to enjoy full run of the house and garden. On the other hand, by letting the newcomer have unrestricted access to the entire household and allowing her to run willy-nilly, she will most certainly develop a bunch of behavior problems in short order, no doubt necessitating confinement later in life. It would not be fair to remedially restrain and confine a dog you have trained, through neglect, to run free.

When confining the dog, make sure she always has an impressive array of suitable chew toys. Kongs and sterilized longbones (both readily available from pet stores) make the best chew toys, since they are hollow and may be stuffed with treats to heighten the dog's interest. For example, by stuffing the little hole at the top of a Kong with a small piece of freeze-dried liver, the dog will not want to leave it alone.

Remember, treats do not have to be junk food and they certainly should not represent extra calories. Rather, treats should be part of each dog's regular daily diet: Some food may be served in the dog's bowl for breakfast and dinner, some food may be used as training treats, and some food may be used for stuffing chew toys. I regularly stuff my dogs' many Kongs with different shaped biscuits and kibble.

Make sure your puppy has suitable chew toys.

The kibble seems to fall out fairly easily, as do the oval-shaped biscuits, thus rewarding the dog instantaneously for checking out the chew toys. The bone-shaped biscuits fall out after a while, rewarding the dog for worrying at the chew toy. But the triangular biscuits never come out. They remain inside the Kong as lures, maintaining the dog's fascination with her chew toy. To further focus the dog's interest, I always make sure to flavor the triangular biscuits by rubbing them with a little cheese or freeze-dried liver.

To teach come, call your dog, open your arms as a welcoming signal, wave a toy or a treat and praise for every step in your direction.

If stuffed chew toys are reserved especially for times the dog is confined, the puppydog will soon learn to enjoy quiet moments in her doggy den and she will quickly develop a chew-toy habit— a good habit! This is a simple *autoshaping* process; all the owner has to do is set up the situation and the dog all but trains herself— easy and effective. Even when the dog is given run of the house, her first inclination will be to indulge her rewarding chew-toy habit rather than destroy less-attractive household articles, such as curtains, carpets, chairs and compact disks. Similarly, a chew-toy chewer will be less inclined to scratch and chew herself excessively. Also, if the dog busies herself as a recreational chewer, she will be less inclined to develop into a recreational barker or digger when left at home alone.

Stuff a number of chew toys whenever the dog is left confined and remove the extra-special-tasting treats when you return. Your dog will now amuse herself with her chew toys before falling asleep and then resume playing with her chew toys when she expects you to return. Since most owner-absent misbehavior happens right after you leave and right before your expected return, your puppydog will now be conveniently preoccupied with her chew toys at these times.

Come and Sit

Most puppies will happily approach virtually anyone, whether called or not; that is, until they collide with adolescence and

develop other more important doggy interests, such as sniffing a multiplicity of exquisite odors on the grass. Your mission, Mr./Ms. Owner, is to teach and reward the pup for coming reliably, willingly and happily when called—and you have just three months to get it done. Unless adequately reinforced, your puppy's tendency to approach people will self-destruct by adolescence.

Call your dog ("Tina, come!"), open your arms (and maybe squat down) as a welcoming signal, waggle a treat or toy as a lure and reward the puppydog when she comes running. Do not wait to praise the dog until she reaches you—she may come 95 percent of the way and then run off after some distraction. Instead, praise the dog's *first* step towards you and continue praising enthusiastically for *every* step she takes in your direction.

When the rapidly approaching puppy dog is three lengths away from impact, instruct her to sit ("Tina, sit!") and hold the lure in front of you in an outstretched hand to prevent her from hitting you midchest and knocking you flat on your back! As Tina decelerates to nose the lure, move the treat upwards and backwards just over her muzzle with an upwards motion of your extended arm (palm-upwards). As the dog looks up to follow the lure, she will sit down (if she jumps up, you are holding the lure too high). Praise the dog for sitting. Move backwards and call her again. Repeat this many times over, always praising when Tina comes and sits; on occasion, reward her.

For the first couple of trials, use a training treat both as a lure to entice the dog to come and sit and as a reward for doing so. Thereafter, try to use different items as lures and rewards. For example, lure the dog with a Kong or Frisbee but reward her with a food treat. Or lure the dog with a food treat but pat her and throw a tennis ball as a reward. After just a few repetitions, dispense with the lures and rewards; the dog will begin to respond willingly to your verbal requests and hand signals just for the prospect of praise from your heart and affection from your hands.

Instruct every family member, friend and visitor how to get the dog to come and sit. Invite people over for a series of pooch parties; do not keep the pup a secret— let other people enjoy this puppy, and let the pup enjoy other people. Puppydog parties are not only fun, they easily attract a lot of people to help *you* train *your* dog. Unless you teach your dog how to meet people, that is, to sit for greetings, no doubt the dog will resort to jumping up. Then you and the visitors will get annoyed, and the dog will be punished. This is not fair. *Send out those invitations for puppy parties and teach your dog to be mannerly and socially acceptable.*

Even though your dog quickly masters obedient recalls in the house, her reliability may falter when playing in the backyard or local park. Ironically, it is *the owner* who has unintentionally trained the dog *not* to respond in these instances. By allowing the dog to play and run around and otherwise have a good time, but then to call the dog to put her on leash to take her home, the dog quickly learns playing is fun but training is a drag. Thus, playing in the park becomes a severe distraction, which works against training. Bad news!

Instead, whether playing with the dog off leash or on leash, request her to come at frequent intervals—say, every minute or so. On most occasions, praise and pet the dog for a few seconds while she is sitting, then tell her to go play again. For especially fast recalls, offer a couple of training treats and take the time to praise and pet the dog enthusiastically before releasing her. The dog will learn that coming when called is not necessarily the end of the play session, and neither is it the end of the world; rather, it signals an enjoyable, quality time-out with the owner before resuming play once more. In fact, playing in the park now becomes a very effective life-reward, which works to facilitate training by reinforcing each obedient and timely recall. Good news!

Sit, Down, Stand and Rollover

Teaching the dog a variety of body positions is easy for owner and dog, impressive for spectators and extremely useful for all. Using lure-reward techniques, it is possible to train several positions at once to verbal commands or hand signals (which impress the socks off onlookers).

Sit and ***down***—the two control commands—prevent or resolve nearly a hundred behavior problems. For example, if the dog happily and obediently sits or lies down when requested, she cannot jump on visitors, dash out the front door, run around and chase her tail, pester other dogs, harass cats or annoy family, friends or strangers. Additionally, "Sit" or "Down" are the best emergency commands for off-leash control.

It is easier to teach and maintain a reliable sit than maintain a reliable recall. *Sit* is the purest and simplest of commands—either the dog is sitting or she is not. If there is any change of circumstances or potential danger in the park, for example, simply instruct the dog to sit. If she sits, you have a number of options: Allow the dog to resume playing when she is safe, walk up and put the dog on leash or call the dog. The dog will be much more likely to come when called if she has already acknowledged her compliance by sitting. If the dog does not sit in the park—train her to!

Stand and ***rollover-stay*** are the two positions for examining the dog. Your veterinarian will love you to distraction if you take a little time to teach the dog to stand still and roll over and play possum. Also, your vet bills will be smaller because it will take the veterinarian less time to examine your dog. The rollover-stay is an especially useful command and is really just a variation of the down-stay: Whereas the dog lies prone in the traditional down, she lies supine in the rollover-stay.

As with teaching come and sit, the training techniques to teach the dog to assume all other body positions on cue are user-friendly and dog-friendly. Simply give the appropriate request, lure the dog into the desired body position using a training treat or toy and then *praise* (and maybe reward) the dog as soon as she complies. Try not to touch the dog to get her to respond. If you teach the dog by guiding her into position, the dog will quickly learn that rump-pressure means sit, for example, but as yet you still have no control over your dog if she is just 6 feet away. It will still be necessary to teach the dog to sit on request. So do not make training a time-consuming two-step process; instead, teach the dog to sit to a verbal request or hand signal from the outset. Once the dog sits willingly when requested, by all means use your hands to pet the dog when she does so.

To teach *down* when the dog is already sitting, say "Tina, down!," hold the lure in one hand (palm down) and lower that hand to the floor between the dog's forepaws. As the dog lowers her head to follow the lure, slowly move the lure away from the dog just a fraction (in front of her paws). The dog will lie down as she stretches her nose forward to follow the lure. Praise the dog when she does so. If the dog stands up, you pulled the lure away too far and too quickly.

When teaching the dog to lie down from the standing position, say "Down" and lower the lure to the floor as before. Once the dog has lowered her forequarters and assumed a play bow, gently and slowly move the lure *towards* the dog between her forelegs. Praise the dog as soon as her rear end plops down.

After just a couple of trials it will be possible to alternate sits and downs and have the dog energetically perform doggy push-ups. Praise the dog a lot, and after half a dozen or so push-ups reward the dog with a training treat or toy. You will notice the more energetically you move your arm—upwards (palm up) to get the dog to sit, and downwards (palm down) to get the dog to lie down—the more energetically the dog responds to your requests. Now try training the dog in silence and you will notice she has also learned to respond to hand signals. Yeah! Not too shabby for the first session.

To teach *stand* from the sitting position, say "Tina, stand," slowly move the lure half a dog-length away from the dog's nose, keeping it at nose level, and praise the dog as she stands to follow the lure. As soon

Using a food lure to teach sit, down and stand. 1) "Phoenix, sit." 2) Hand palm upwards, move lure up and back over dog's muzzle. 3) "Good sit, Phoenix!" 4) "Phoenix, down." 5) Hand palm downwards, move lure down to lie between dog's forepaws. 6) "Phoenix, off. Good down, Phoenix!" 7) "Phoenix, sit!" 8) Palm upwards, move lure up and back, keeping it close to dog's muzzle. 9) "Good sit, Phoenix!"

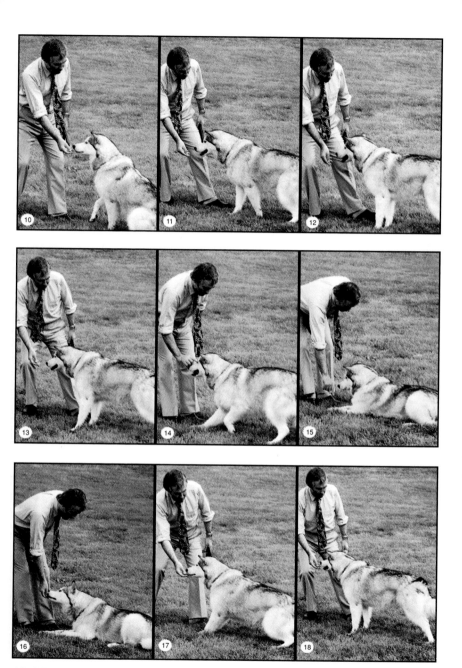

10) *"Phoenix, stand!"* 11) *Move lure away from dog at nose height, then lower it a tad.* 12) *"Phoenix, off! Good stand, Phoenix!"* 13) *"Phoenix, down!"* 14) *Hand palm downwards, move lure down to lie between dog's forepaws.* 15) *"Phoenix, off! Good down-stay, Phoenix!"* 16) *"Phoenix, stand!"* 17) *Move lure away from dog's muzzle up to nose height.* 18) *"Phoenix, off! Good stand-stay, Phoenix. Now we'll make the vet and groomer happy!"*

as the dog stands, lower the lure to just beneath the dog's chin to entice her to look down; otherwise she will stand and then sit immediately. To prompt the dog to stand from the down position, move the lure half a dog-length upwards and away from the dog, holding the lure at standing nose height from the floor.

Teaching *rollover* is best started from the down position, with the dog lying on one side, or at least with both hind legs stretched out on the same side. Say "Tina, bang!" and move the lure backwards and alongside the dog's muzzle to her elbow (on the side of her outstretched hind legs). Once the dog looks to the side and backwards, very slowly move the lure upwards to the dog's shoulder and backbone. Tickling the dog in the goolies (groin area) often invokes a reflex-raising of the hind leg as an appeasement gesture, which facilitates the tendency to roll over. If you move the lure too quickly and the dog jumps into the standing position, have patience and start again. As soon as the dog rolls onto her back, keep the lure stationary and mesmerize the dog with a relaxing tummy rub.

To teach *rollover-stay* when the dog is standing or moving, say "Tina, bang!" and give the appropriate hand signal (with index finger pointed and thumb cocked in true Sam Spade fashion), then in one fluid movement lure her to first lie down and then rollover-stay as above.

Teaching the dog to *stay* in each of the above four positions becomes a piece of cake after first teaching the dog not to worry at the toy or treat training lure. This is best accomplished by hand feeding dinner kibble. Hold a piece of kibble firmly in your hand and softly instruct "Off!" Ignore any licking and slobbering *for however long the dog worries at the treat*, but say "Take it!" and offer the kibble *the instant* the dog breaks contact with her muzzle. Repeat this a few times, and then up the ante and insist the dog remove her muzzle for one whole second before offering the kibble. Then progressively refine your criteria and have the dog not touch your hand (or treat) for longer and longer periods on each trial, such as for two seconds, four seconds, then six, ten, fifteen, twenty, thirty seconds and so on.

The dog soon learns: (1) worrying at the treat never gets results, whereas (2) noncontact is often rewarded after a variable time lapse.

Teaching *"Off!"* has many useful applications in its own right. Additionally, instructing the dog not to touch a training lure often produces spontaneous and magical stays. Request the dog to stand-stay, for example, and not to touch the lure. At first set your sights on a short two-second stay before rewarding the dog. (Remember, every long journey begins with a single step.) However, on subsequent trials, gradually and progressively increase the length of stay required to receive a reward. In no time at all your dog will stand calmly for a minute or so.

Relevancy Training

Once you have taught the dog what you expect her to do when requested to come, sit, lie down, stand, roll-over and stay, the time is right to teach the dog *why* she should comply with your wishes. The secret is to have many (*many*) extremely short training interludes (two to five seconds each) at numerous (*numerous*) times during the course of the dog's day. Especially work with the dog immediately *before* the dog's good times and *during* the dog's good times. For example, ask your dog to sit and/or lie down each time before opening doors, serving meals, offering treats and tummy rubs; ask the dog to perform a few controlled doggy push-ups before letting her off leash or throwing a tennis ball; and perhaps request the dog to sit-down-sit-stand-down-stand-rollover before inviting her to cuddle on the couch.

Similarly, request the dog to sit many times during play or on walks, and in no time at all the dog will be only too pleased to follow your instructions because she has learned that a compliant response heralds all sorts of goodies. Basically all you are trying to teach the dog is how to say please: "Please throw the tennis ball. Please may I snuggle on the couch."

Remember, it is important to keep training interludes short and to have many short sessions each and every day. The shortest (and most useful) session comprises asking the dog to sit and then go play during a play session. When trained this way, your dog will soon associate training with good times. In fact, the dog may be unable to distinguish between training and good times and, indeed, there should be no distinction. The warped concept that training involves forcing the dog to comply and/or dominating her will is totally at odds with the picture of a truly well-trained dog. In reality, enjoying a game of training with a dog is no different from enjoying a game of backgammon or tennis with a friend; and walking with a dog should be no different from strolling with a spouse, or with buddies on the golf course.

Walk by Your Side

Many people attempt to teach a dog to heel by putting her on a leash and physically correcting the dog when she makes mistakes. There are a number of things seriously wrong with this approach, the first being that most people do not want precision heeling; rather, they simply want the dog to follow or walk by their side. Second, when physically restrained during "training," even though the dog may grudgingly mope by your side when "handcuffed" on leash, let's see what happens when she is off leash. History! The dog is in the next county because she never enjoyed walking with you on leash and you have no control over her off leash. So let's just teach the dog off leash from the outset to *want* to walk with us. Third, if the dog has not been trained to heel, it is a trifle hasty to think about punishing the poor dog for making mistakes and breaking heeling rules she didn't even know existed. This is simply not fair! Surely, if the dog had been adequately taught how to heel, she would seldom make mistakes and hence there would be no need to correct the dog. Remember, each mistake and each correction (punishment) advertise the trainer's inadequacy, not the dog's. The dog is not stubborn, she is not stupid and she is not bad. Even if she were, she would still require training, so let's train her properly.

Let's teach the dog to *enjoy* following us and to *want* to walk by our side off leash. Then it will be easier to teach high-precision off-leash heeling patterns if desired. Before going on outdoor walks, it is necessary to teach the dog not to pull. Then it becomes easy to teach on-leash walking and heeling because the dog already wants to walk with you, she is familiar with the desired walking and heeling positions and she knows not to pull.

FOLLOWING

Start by training your dog to follow you. Many puppies will follow if you simply walk away from them and maybe click your fingers or chuckle. Adult dogs may require additional enticement to stimulate them to follow, such as a training lure or, at the very least, a lively trainer. To teach the dog to follow: (1) keep walking and (2) walk away from the dog. If the dog attempts to lead or lag, change pace; slow down if the dog forges too far ahead, but speed up if she lags too far behind. Say "Steady!" or "Easy!" each time before you slow down and "Quickly!" or "Hustle!" each time before you speed up, and the dog will learn to change pace on cue. If the dog lags or leads too far, or if she wanders right or left, simply walk quickly in the opposite direction and maybe even run away from the dog and hide.

Practicing is a lot of fun; you can set up a course in your home, yard or park to do this. Indoors, entice the dog to follow upstairs, into a bedroom, into the bathroom, downstairs, around the living room couch, zigzagging between dining room chairs and into the kitchen for dinner. Outdoors, get the dog to follow around park benches, trees, shrubs and along walkways and lines in the grass. (For safety outdoors, it is advisable to attach a long line on the dog, but never exert corrective tension on the line.)

Remember, following has a lot to do with attitude—*your* attitude! Most probably your dog will *not* want to follow Mr. Grumpy Troll with the personality of wilted lettuce. Lighten up—walk with a jaunty step, whistle a happy tune, sing, skip and tell jokes to your dog and she will be right there by your side.

BY YOUR SIDE

It is smart to train the dog to walk close on one side or the other—either side will do, your choice. When walking, jogging or cycling, it is generally bad news to have the dog suddenly cut in front of you. In fact, I train my dogs to walk "By my side" and "Other side"—both very useful instructions. It is possible to position the dog fairly accurately by looking to the appropriate side and clicking your fingers or slapping your thigh on that side. A precise positioning may be attained by holding a training lure, such as a chew toy, tennis ball or food treat. Stop and stand still several times throughout the walk, just as you would when window shopping or meeting a friend. Use the lure to make sure the dog slows down and stays close whenever you stop.

When teaching the dog to heel, we generally want her to sit in heel position when we stop. Teach heel

Using a toy to teach sit-heel-sit sequences: 1) "Phoenix, sit!" Standing still, move lure up and back over dog's muzzle . . . 2) to position dog sitting in heel position on your left side. 3) Say "Phoenix, heel!" and walk ahead, wagging lure in left hand. Change lure to right hand in preparation for sit signal. Say "Sit" and then . . .

position at the standstill and the dog will learn that the default heel position is sitting by your side (left or right—your choice, unless you wish to compete in obedience trials, in which case the dog must heel on the left).

Several times a day, stand up and call your dog to come and sit in heel position—"Tina, heel!" For example, instruct the dog to come to heel each time there are commercials on TV, or each time you turn a page of a novel, and the dog will get it in a single evening.

Practice straight-line heeling and turns separately. With the dog sitting at heel, teach her to turn in place. After each quarter-turn, half-turn or full turn in place, lure the dog to sit at heel. Now it's time for short straight-line heeling sequences, no more than a few steps at a time. Always think of heeling in terms of sit-heel-sit sequences—start and end with the dog in position and do your best to keep her there when moving. Progressively increase the number of steps in each sequence. When the dog remains close for 20 yards of straight-line heeling, it is time to add a few turns and then sign up for a happy-heeling obedience class to get some advice from the experts.

4) use hand signal to lure dog to sit as you stop. Eventually, dog will sit automatically at heel whenever you stop. 5) "Good dog!"

No Pulling on Leash

You can start teaching your dog not to pull on leash anywhere—in front of the television or outdoors—but regardless of location, you must not take a single step with tension in the leash. For a reason known only to dogs, even just a couple of paces of pulling on leash is intrinsically motivating and diabolically rewarding. Instead, attach the leash to the dog's collar, grasp the other end firmly with both hands held close to your chest, and stand still—do not budge an inch. Have somebody watch you with a stopwatch to time your progress, or else you will never believe this will work and so you will not even try the exercise, and your shoulder and the dog's neck will be traumatized for years to come.

Stand still and wait for the dog to stop pulling, and to sit and/or lie down. All dogs stop pulling and sit eventually. Most take only a couple of minutes; the all-time record is 22½ minutes. Time how long it takes. Gently praise the dog when she stops pulling, and as soon as she sits, enthusiastically praise the dog and take just one step forward, then immediately stand still. This single step usually demonstrates the ballistic reinforcing nature of pulling on leash; most dogs explode to the end of the leash, so be prepared for the strain. Stand firm and wait for the dog to sit again. Repeat this half a dozen times and you will probably notice a progressive reduction in the force of the dog's one-step explosions and a radical reduction in the time it takes for the dog to sit each time.

As the dog learns "Sit we go" and "Pull we stop," she will begin to walk forward calmly with each single step and automatically sit when you stop. Now try two steps before you stop. Woooooooo! Scary! When the dog has mastered two steps at a time, try for three. After each success, progressively increase the number of steps in the sequence: try four steps and then six, eight, ten and twenty steps before stopping. Congratulations! You are now walking the dog on leash.

Whenever walking with the dog (off leash or on leash), make sure you stop periodically to practice a few position commands and stays before instructing the dog to "Walk on!" (Remember, you want the dog to be compliant everywhere, not just in the kitchen when her dinner is at hand.) For example, stopping every 25 yards to briefly train the dog amounts to over 200 training interludes within a single 3-mile stroll. And each training session is in a different location. You will not believe the improvement within just the first mile of the first walk.

To put it another way, integrating training into a walk offers 200 separate opportunities to use the continuance of the walk as a reward to reinforce the dog's education. Moreover, some training interludes may comprise continuing education for the dog's walking skills: Alternate short periods of the dog walking calmly by your side with periods when the dog is allowed to sniff and investigate the environment. Now sniffing odors on the grass and meeting other dogs become rewards which reinforce the dog's calm and mannerly demeanor. Good Lord! Whatever next? Many enjoyable walks together of course. Happy trails!

THE IMPORTANCE OF TRICKS

Nothing will improve a dog's quality of life better than having a few tricks under her belt. Teaching any trick expands the dog's vocabulary, which facilitates communication and improves the owner's control. Also, specific tricks help prevent and resolve specific behavior problems. For example, by teaching the dog to fetch her toys, the dog learns carrying a toy makes the owner happy and, therefore, will be more likely to chew her toy than other inappropriate items.

More important, teaching tricks prompts owners to lighten up and train with a sunny disposition. Really, tricks should be no different from any other behaviors we put on cue. But they are. When teaching tricks, owners have a much sweeter attitude, which in turn motivates the dog and improves her willingness to comply. The dog feels tricks are a blast, but formal commands are a drag. In fact, tricks are so enjoyable, they may be used as rewards in training by asking the dog to come, sit and down-stay and then rollover for a tummy rub. Go on, try it: Crack a smile and even giggle when the dog promptly and willingly lies down and stays.

Most important, performing tricks prompts onlookers to smile and giggle. Many people are scared of dogs, especially large ones. And nothing can be more off-putting for a dog than to be constantly confronted by strangers who don't like her because of her size or the way she looks. Uneasy people put the dog on edge, causing her to back off and bark, only frightening people all the more. And so a vicious circle develops, with the people's fear fueling the dog's fear *and vice versa*. Instead, tie a pink ribbon to your dog's collar and practice all sorts of tricks on walks and in the park, and you will be pleasantly amazed how it changes people's attitudes toward your friendly dog. The dog's repertoire of tricks is limited only by the trainer's imagination. Below I have described three of my favorites:

SPEAK AND SHUSH

The training sequence involved in teaching a dog to bark on request is no different from that used when training any behavior on cue: request—lure—response—reward. As always, the secret of success lies in finding an effective lure. If the dog always barks at the doorbell, for example, say "Rover, speak!", have an accomplice ring the doorbell, then reward the dog for barking. After a few woofs, ask Rover to "Shush!", waggle a food treat under her nose (to entice her to sniff and thus to shush), praise her when quiet and eventually offer the treat as a reward. Alternate "Speak" and "Shush," progressively increasing the length of shush-time between each barking bout.

PLAY BOW

With the dog standing, say "Bow!" and lower the food lure (palm upwards) to rest between the dog's forepaws. Praise as the dog lowers

her forequarters and sternum to the ground (as when teaching the down), but then lure the dog to stand and offer the treat. On successive trials, gradually increase the length of time the dog is required to remain in the play bow posture in order to gain a food reward. If the dog's rear end collapses into a down, say nothing and offer no reward; simply start over.

BE A BEAR

With the dog sitting backed into a corner to prevent her from toppling over backwards, say "Be a bear!" With bent paw and palm down, raise a lure upwards and backwards along the top of the dog's muzzle. Praise the dog when she sits up on her haunches and offer the treat as a reward. To prevent the dog from standing on her hind legs, keep the lure closer to the dog's muzzle. On each trial, progressively increase the length of time the dog is required to sit up to receive a food reward. Since lure-reward training is so easy, teach the dog to stand and walk on her hind legs as well!

Teaching "Be a Bear"

chapter 9

Getting
Active
with your Dog
by Bardi McLennan

Once you and your dog have graduated from basic obedience training and are beginning to work together as a team, you can take part in the growing world of dog activities. There are so many fun things to do with your dog! Just remember, people and dogs don't always learn at the same pace, so don't be upset if you (or your dog) need more than two basic training courses before your team becomes operational. Even smart dogs don't go straight to college from kindergarten!

Just as there are events geared to certain types of dogs, so there are ones that are more appealing to certain types of people. In some

128

activities, you give the commands and your dog does the work (upland game hunting is one example), while in others, such as agility, you'll both get a workout. You may want to aim for prestigious titles to add to your dog's name, or you may want nothing more than the sheer enjoyment of being around other people and their dogs. Passive or active, participation has its own rewards.

Consider your dog's physical capabilities when looking into any of the canine activities. It's easy to see that a Basset Hound is not built for the racetrack, nor would a Chihuahua be the breed of choice for pulling a sled. A loyal dog will attempt almost anything you ask him to do, so it is up to you to know your dog's limitations. A dog must be physically sound in order to compete at any level in athletic activities, and being mentally sound is a definite plus. Advanced age, however, may not be a deterrent. Many dogs still hunt and herd at ten or twelve years of age. It's entirely possible for dogs to be "fit at 50." Take your dog for a checkup, explain to your vet the type of activity you have in mind and be guided by his or her findings.

All dogs seem to love playing flyball.

You needn't be restricted to breed-specific sports if it's only fun you're after. Certain AKC activities are limited to designated breeds; however, as each new trial, test or sport has grown in popularity, so has the variety of breeds encouraged to participate at a fun level.

But don't shortchange your fun, or that of your dog, by thinking only of the basic function of her breed. Once a dog has learned how to learn, she can be taught to do just about anything as long as the size of the dog is right for the job and you both think it is fun and rewarding. In other words, you are a team.

To get involved in any of the activities detailed in this chapter, look for the names and addresses of the organizations that sponsor them in Chapter 13. You can also ask your breeder or a local dog trainer for contacts.

You can compete in obedience trials with a well trained dog.

Official American Kennel Club Activities

The following tests and trials are some of the events sanctioned by the AKC and sponsored by various dog clubs. Your dog's expertise will be rewarded with impressive titles. You can participate just for fun, or be competitive and go for those awards.

OBEDIENCE

Training classes begin with pups as young as three months of age in kindergarten puppy training, then advance to pre-novice (all exercises on lead) and go on to novice, which is where you'll start off-lead work. In obedience classes dogs learn to sit, stay, heel and come through a variety of exercises. Once you've got the basics down, you can enter obedience trials and work toward earning your dog's first degree, a C.D. (Companion Dog).

The next level is called "Open," in which jumps and retrieves perk up the dog's interest. Passing grades in competition at this level earn a C.D.X. (Companion Dog Excellent). Beyond that lies the goal of the most ambitious—Utility (U.D. and even U.D.X. or OTCh, an Obedience Champion).

AGILITY

All dogs can participate in the latest canine sport to have gained worldwide popularity for its fun and excitement, agility. It began in England as a canine version of horse show-jumping, but because dogs are more agile and able to perform on verbal commands, extra feats were added such as climbing, balancing and racing through tunnels or in and out of weave poles. Many of the obstacles (regulation or homemade) can be set up in your own backyard. If the agility bug bites, you could end up in international competition!

For starters, your dog should be obedience trained, even though, in the beginning, the lessons may all be taught on lead. Once the dog understands the commands (and you do, too), it's as easy as guiding the dog over a prescribed course, one obstacle at a time. In competition, the race is against the clock, so wear your running shoes! The dog starts with 200 points and the judge deducts for infractions and misadventures along the way.

All dogs seem to love agility and respond to it as if they were being turned loose in a playground paradise. Your dog's enthusiasm will be contagious; agility turns into great fun for dog and owner.

FIELD TRIALS AND HUNTING TESTS

There are field trials and hunting tests for the sporting breeds—retrievers, spaniels and pointing breeds, and for some hounds—Bassets, Beagles and Dachshunds. Field trials are competitive events that test a dog's ability to perform the functions for which she was bred. Hunting tests, which are open to retrievers,

---

TITLES AWARDED BY THE AKC

Conformation: Ch. (Champion)

Obedience: CD (Companion Dog); CDX (Companion Dog Excellent); UD (Utility Dog); UDX (Utility Dog Excellent); OTCh. (Obedience Trial Champion)

Field: JH (Junior Hunter); SH (Senior Hunter); MH (Master Hunter); AFCh. (Amateur Field Champion); FCh. (Field Champion)

Lure Coursing: JC (Junior Courser); SC (Senior Courser)

Herding: HT (Herding Tested); PT (Pre-Trial Tested); HS (Herding Started); HI (Herding Intermediate); HX (Herding Excellent); HCh. (Herding Champion)

Tracking: TD (Tracking Dog); TDX (Tracking Dog Excellent)

Agility: NAD (Novice Agility); OAD (Open Agility); ADX (Agility Excellent); MAX (Master Agility)

Earthdog Tests: JE (Junior Earthdog); SE (Senior Earthdog); ME (Master Earthdog)

Canine Good Citizen: CGC

Combination: DC (Dual Champion—Ch. and Fch.); TC (Triple Champion—Ch., Fch., and OTCh.)

spaniels and pointing breeds only, are noncompetitive and are a means of judging the dog's ability as well as that of the handler.

Hunting is a very large and complex part of canine sports, and if you own one of the breeds that hunts, the events are a great treat for your dog and you. He gets to do what he was bred for, and you get to work with him and watch him do it. You'll be proud of and amazed at what your dog can do.

Fortunately, the AKC publishes a series of booklets on these events, which outline the rules and regulations and include a glossary of the sometimes complicated terms. The AKC also publishes newsletters for field trialers and hunting test enthusiasts. The United Kennel Club (UKC) also has informative materials for the hunter and his dog.

Retrievers and other sporting breeds get to do what they're bred to in hunting tests.

HERDING TESTS AND TRIALS

Herding, like hunting, dates back to the first known uses man made of dogs. The interest in herding today is widespread, and if you own a herding breed, you can join in the activity. Herding dogs are tested for their natural skills to keep a flock of ducks, sheep or cattle together. If your dog shows potential, you can start at the testing level, where your dog can earn a title for showing an inherent herding ability. With training you can advance to the trial level, where your dog should be capable of controlling even difficult livestock in diverse situations.

LURE COURSING

The AKC Tests and Trials for Lure Coursing are open to traditional sighthounds—Greyhounds, Whippets,

Borzoi, Salukis, Afghan Hounds, Ibizan Hounds and Scottish Deerhounds—as well as to Basenjis and Rhodesian Ridgebacks. Hounds are judged on overall ability, follow, speed, agility and endurance. This is possibly the most exciting of the trials for spectators, because the speed and agility of the dogs is awesome to watch as they chase the lure (or "course") in heats of two or three dogs at a time.

TRACKING

Tracking is another activity in which almost any dog can compete because every dog that sniffs the ground when taken outdoors is, in fact, tracking. The hard part comes when the rules as to what, when and where the dog tracks are determined by a person, not the dog! Tracking tests cover a large area of fields, woods and roads. The tracks are laid hours before the dogs go to work on them, and include "tricks" like cross-tracks and sharp turns. If you're interested in search-and-rescue work, this is the place to start.

This tracking dog is hot on the trail.

EARTHDOG TESTS FOR SMALL TERRIERS AND DACHSHUNDS

These tests are open to Australian, Bedlington, Border, Cairn, Dandie Dinmont, Smooth and Wire Fox, Lakeland, Norfolk, Norwich, Scottish, Sealyham, Skye, Welsh and West Highland White Terriers as well as Dachshunds. The dogs need no prior training for this terrier sport. There is a qualifying test on the day of the event, so dog and handler learn the rules on the spot. These tests, or "digs," sometimes end with informal races in the late afternoon.

133

Here are some of the extracurricular obedience and racing activities that are not regulated by the AKC or UKC, but are generally run by clubs or a group of dog fanciers and are often open to all.

Canine Freestyle This activity is something new on the scene and is variously likened to dancing, dressage or ice skating. It is meant to show the athleticism of the dog, but also requires showmanship on the part of the dog's handler. If you and your dog like to ham it up for friends, you might want to look into freestyle.

Lure coursing lets sighthounds do what they do best—run!

Scent Hurdle Racing Scent hurdle racing is purely a fun activity sponsored by obedience clubs with members forming competing teams. The height of the hurdles is based on the size of the shortest dog on the team. On a signal, one team dog is released on each of two side-by-side courses and must clear every hurdle before picking up its own dumbbell from a platform and returning over the jumps to the handler. As each dog returns, the next on that team is sent. Of course, that is what the dogs are supposed to do. When the dogs improvise (going under or around the hurdles, stealing another dog's dumbbell, and so forth), it no doubt frustrates the handlers, but just adds to the fun for everyone else.

Flyball This type of racing is similar, but after negotiating the four hurdles, the dog comes to a flyball box, steps on a lever that releases a tennis ball into the air, catches the ball and returns over the hurdles to the starting point. This game also becomes extremely fun for spectators because the dogs sometimes cheat by catching a ball released by the dog in the next lane. Three titles can be earned—Flyball Dog (F.D.), Flyball Dog Excellent (F.D.X.) and Flyball Dog Champion (Fb.D.Ch.)—all awarded by the North American Flyball Association, Inc.

Dogsledding The name conjures up the Rocky Mountains or the frigid North, but you can find dogsled clubs in such unlikely spots as Maryland, North Carolina and Virginia! Dogsledding is primarily for the Nordic breeds such as the Alaskan Malamutes, Siberian Huskies and Samoyeds, but other breeds can try. There are some practical backyard applications to this sport, too. With parental supervision, almost any strong dog could pull a child's sled.

Coming over the A-frame on an agility course.

These are just some of the many recreational ways you can get to know and understand your multifaceted dog better and have fun doing it.

chapter 10

Your Dog
and your
Family

by Bardi McLennan

Adding a dog automatically increases your family by one, no matter whether you live alone in an apartment or are part of a mother, father and six kids household. The single-person family is fair game for numerous and varied canine misconceptions as to who is dog and who pays the bills, whereas a dog in a houseful of children will consider himself to be just one of the gang, littermates all. One dog and one child may give a dog reason to believe they are both kids or both dogs. Either interpretation requires parental supervision and sometimes speedy intervention.

As soon as one paw goes through the door into your home, Rufus (or Rufina) has to make many adjustments to become a part of your family. Your job is to make him fit in as painlessly as possible. An older dog may have some frame of reference from past experience, but to a 10-week-old puppy, everything is brand new: people, furniture, stairs, when and where people eat, sleep or watch TV, his own place and everyone else's space, smells, sounds, outdoors—everything!

Puppies, and newly acquired dogs of any age, do not need what we think of as "freedom." If you leave a new dog or puppy loose in the house, you will almost certainly return to chaotic destruction and the dog will forever after equate your homecoming with a time of punishment to be dreaded. It is unfair to give your dog what amounts to "freedom to get into trouble." Instead, confine him to a crate for brief periods of your absence (up to three or four hours) and, for the long haul, a workday for example, confine him to one untrashable area with his own toys, a bowl of water and a radio left on (low) in another room.

Lots of pets get along with each other just fine.

For the first few days, when not confined, put Rufus on a long leash tied to your wrist or waist. This umbilical cord method enables the dog to learn all about you from your body language and voice, and to learn by his own actions which things in the house are NO! and which ones are rewarded by "Good dog." House-training will be easier with the pup always by your side. Speaking of which, accidents do happen. That goal of "completely housetrained" takes up to a year, or the length of time it takes the pup to mature.

The All-Adult Family

Most dogs in an adults-only household today are likely to be latchkey pets, with no one home all day but the dog. When you return after a tough day on the job, the dog can and should be your relaxation therapy. But going home can instead be a daily frustration.

Separation anxiety is a very common problem for the dog in a working household. It may begin with whines and barks of loneliness, but it will soon escalate into a frenzied destruction derby. That is why it is so important to set aside the time to teach a dog to relax when left alone in his confined area and to understand that he can trust you to return.

Let the dog get used to your work schedule in easy stages. Confine him to one room and go in and out of that room over and over again. Be casual about it. No physical, voice or eye contact. When the pup no longer even notices your comings and goings, leave the house for varying lengths of time, returning to stay home for a few minutes and gradually increasing the time away. This training can take days, but the dog is learning that you haven't left him forever and that he can trust you.

Any time you leave the dog, but especially during this training period, be casual about your departure. No anxiety-building fond farewells. Just "Bye" and go! Remember the "Good dog" when you return to find everything more or less as you left it.

If things are a mess (or even a disaster) when you return, greet the dog, take him outside to eliminate, and then put him in his crate while you clean up. Rant and rave in the shower! *Do not* punish the dog. You were not there when it happened, and the rule is: Only punish as you catch the dog in the act of wrongdoing. Obviously, it makes sense to get your latchkey puppy when you'll have a week or two to spend on these training essentials.

Family weekend activities should include Rufus whenever possible. Depending on the pup's age, now is the time for a long walk in the park, playtime in the backyard, a hike in the woods. Socializing is as important as health care, good food and physical exercise, so visiting Aunt Emma or Uncle Harry and the next-door neighbor's dog or cat is essential to developing an outgoing, friendly temperament in your pet.

If you are a single adult, socializing Rufus at home and away will prevent him from becoming overly protective of you (or just overly attached) and will also prevent such behavioral problems as dominance or fear of strangers.

Babies

Whether already here or on the way, babies figure larger than life in the eyes of a dog. If the dog is there first, let him in on all your baby preparations in the house. When baby arrives, let Rufus sniff any item of clothing that has been on the baby before Junior comes home. Then let Mom greet the dog first before introducing the new family member. Hold the baby down for the dog to see and sniff, but make sure some-

one's holding the dog on lead in case of any sudden moves. Don't play keep-away or tease the dog with the baby, which only invites undesirable jumping up.

The dog and the baby are "family," and for starters can be treated almost as equals. Things rapidly change, however, especially when baby takes to creeping around on all fours on the dog's turf or, better yet, has yummy pudding all over her face and hands! That's when a lot of things in the dog's and baby's lives become more separate than equal.

Dogs are perfect confidants.

Toddlers make terrible dog owners, but if you can't avoid the combination, use patient discipline (that is, positive teaching rather than punishment), and use time-outs before you run out of patience.

A dog and a baby (or toddler, or an assertive young child) should never be left alone together. Take the dog with you or confine him. With a baby or youngsters in the house, you'll have plenty of use for that wonderful canine safety device called a crate!

Young Children

Any dog in a house with kids will behave pretty much as the kids do, good or bad. But even good dogs and good children can get into trouble when play becomes rowdy and active.

Legs bobbing up and down, shrill voices screeching, a ball hurtling overhead, all add up to exuberant frustration for a dog who's just trying to be part of the gang. In a pack of puppies, any legs or toys being chased would be caught by a set of teeth, and all the pups involved would understand that is how the game is played. Kids do not understand this, nor do parents tolerate it. Bring Rufus indoors before you have reason to regret it. This is time-out, not a punishment.

Teach children how to play nicely with a puppy.

You can explain the situation to the children and tell them they must play quieter games until the puppy learns not to grab them with his mouth. Unfortunately, you can't explain it that easily to the dog. With adult supervision, they will learn how to play together.

Young children love to tease. Sticking their faces or wiggling their hands or fingers in the dog's face is teasing. To another person it might be just annoying, but it is threatening to a dog. There's another difference: We can make the child stop by an explanation, but the only way a dog can stop it is with a warning growl and then with teeth. Teasing is the major cause of children being bitten by their pets. Treat it seriously.

Older Children

The best age for a child to get a first dog is between the ages of 8 and 12. That's when kids are able to accept some real responsibility for their pet. Even so, take the child's vow of "I will never *ever* forget to feed (brush, walk, etc.) the dog" for what it's worth: a child's good intention at that moment. Most kids today have extra lessons, soccer practice, Little League, ballet, and so forth piled on top of school schedules. There will be many times when Mom will have to come to the dog's rescue. "I walked the dog for you so you can set the table for me" is one way to get around a missed appointment without laying on blame or guilt.

Kids in this age group make excellent obedience trainers because they are into the teaching/learning process themselves and they lack the self-consciousness of adults. Attending a dog show is something the whole family can enjoy, and watching Junior Showmanship may catch the eye of the kids. Older children can begin to get involved in many of the recreational activities that were reviewed in the previous chapter. Some of the agility obstacles, for example, can be set up in the backyard as a family project (with an adult making sure all the equipment is safe and secure for the dog).

Older kids are also beginning to look to the future, and may envision themselves as veterinarians or trainers or show dog handlers or writers of the next Lassie best-seller. Dogs are perfect confidants for these dreams. They won't tell a soul.

Other Pets

Introduce all pets tactfully. In a dog/cat situation, hold the dog, not the cat. Let two dogs meet on neutral turf—a stroll in the park or a walk down the street—with both on loose leads to permit all the normal canine ways of saying hello, including routine sniffing, circling, more sniffing, and so on. Small creatures such as hamsters, chinchillas or mice must be kept safe from their natural predators (dogs and cats).

Festive Family Occasions

Parties are great for people, but not necessarily for puppies. Until all the guests have arrived, put the dog in his crate or in a room where he won't be disturbed. A socialized dog can join the fun later as long as he's not underfoot, annoying guests or into the hors d'oeuvres.

There are a few dangers to consider, too. Doors opening and closing can allow a puppy to slip out unnoticed in the confusion, and you'll be organizing a search party instead of playing host or hostess. Party food and buffet service are not for dogs. Let Rufus party in his crate with a nice big dog biscuit.

At Christmas time, not only are tree decorations dangerous and breakable (and perhaps family heirlooms), but extreme caution should be taken with the lights, cords and outlets for the tree lights and any other festive lighting. Occasionally a dog lifts a leg, ignoring the fact that the tree is indoors. To avoid this, use a canine repellent, made for gardens, on the tree. Or keep him out of the tree room unless supervised. And whatever you do, *don't* invite trouble by hanging his toys on the tree!

Car Travel

Before you plan a vacation by car or RV with Rufus, be sure he enjoys car travel. Nothing spoils a holiday quicker than a carsick dog! Work within the dog's comfort level. Get in the car with the dog in his crate or attached to a canine car safety belt and just sit there until he relaxes. That's all. Next time, get in the car, turn on the engine and go nowhere. Just sit. When that is okay, turn on the engine and go around the block. Now you can go for a ride and include a stop where you get out, leaving the dog for a minute or two.

On a warm day, always park in the shade and leave windows open several inches. And return quickly. It only takes 10 minutes for a car to become an overheated steel death trap.

Motel or Pet Motel?

Not all motels or hotels accept pets, but you have a much better choice today than even a few years ago. To find a dog-friendly lodging, look at *On the Road Again With Man's Best Friend*, a series of directories that detail bed and breakfasts, inns, family resorts and other hotels/motels. Some places require a refundable deposit to cover any damage incurred by the dog. More B&Bs accept pets now, but some restrict the size.

If taking Rufus with you is not feasible, check out boarding kennels in your area. Your veterinarian may offer this service, or recommend a kennel or two he or she is familiar with. Go see the facilities for yourself, ask about exercise, diet, housing, and so on. Or, if you'd rather have Rufus stay home, look into bonded petsitters, many of whom will also bring in the mail and water your plants.

chapter 11

Your Dog
and your
Community

by Bardi McLennan

Step outside your home with your dog and you are no longer just family, you are both part of your community. This is when the phrase "responsible pet ownership" takes on serious implications. For starters, it means you pick up after your dog—not just occasionally, but every time your dog eliminates away from home. That means you have joined the Plastic Baggy Brigade! You always have plastic sandwich bags in your pocket and several in the car. It means you teach your kids how to use them, too. If you think this is "yucky," just imagine what the person (a non-doggy person) who inadvertently steps in the mess thinks!

Your responsibility extends to your neighbors: To their ears (no annoying barking); to their property (their garbage, their lawn, their flower beds, their cat—especially their cat); to their kids (on bikes, at play); to their kids' toys and sports equipment.

There are numerous dog-related laws, ranging from simple dog licensing and leash laws to those holding you liable for any physical injury or property damage done by your dog. These laws are in place to protect everyone in the community, including you and your dog. There are town ordinances and state laws which are by no means the same in all towns or all states. Ignorance of the law won't get you off the hook. The time to find out what the laws are where you live is now.

Be sure your dog's license is current. This is not just a good local ordinance, it can make the difference between finding your lost dog or not.

Dressing your dog up makes him appealing to strangers.

Many states now require proof of rabies vaccination and that the dog has been spayed or neutered before issuing a license. At the same time, keep up the dog's annual immunizations.

Never let your dog run loose in the neighborhood. This will not only keep you on the right side of the leash law, it's the outdoor version of the rule about not giving your dog "freedom to get into trouble."

Good Canine Citizen

Sometimes it's hard for a dog's owner to assess whether or not the dog is sufficiently socialized to be accepted by the community at large. Does Rufus or Rufina display good, controlled behavior in public? The AKC's Canine Good Citizen program is available through many dog organizations. If your dog passes the test, the title "CGC" is earned.

The overall purpose is to turn your dog into a good neighbor and to teach you about your responsibility to your community as a dog owner. Here are the ten things your dog must do willingly:

1. Accept a stranger stopping to chat with you.
2. Sit and be petted by a stranger.
3. Allow a stranger to handle him or her as a groomer or veterinarian would.
4. Walk nicely on a loose lead.
5. Walk calmly through a crowd.
6. Sit and down on command, then stay in a sit or down position while you walk away.
7. Come when called.
8. Casually greet another dog.
9. React confidently to distractions.
10. Accept being left alone with someone other than you and not become overly agitated or nervous.

Schools and Dogs

Schools are getting involved with pet ownership on an educational level. It has been proven that children who are kind to animals are humane in their attitude toward other people as adults.

A dog is a child's best friend, and so children are often primary pet owners, if not the primary caregivers. Unfortunately, they are also the ones most often bitten by dogs. This occurs due to a lack of understanding that pets, no matter how sweet, cuddly and loving, are still animals. Schools, along with parents, dog clubs, dog fanciers and the AKC, are working to change all that with video programs for children not only in grade school, but in the nursery school and pre-kindergarten age group. Teaching youngsters how to be responsible dog owners is important community work. When your dog has a CGC, volunteer to take part in an educational classroom event put on by your dog club.

Boy Scout Merit Badge

A Merit Badge for Dog Care can be earned by any Boy
Scout ages 11 to 18. The requirements are not easy, but
amount to a complete course in responsible dog care
and general ownership. Here are just a few of the
things a Scout must do to earn that badge:

Point out ten parts of the dog using the correct
names.

Give a report (signed by parent or guardian) on
your care of the dog (feeding, food used, housing,
exercising, grooming and bathing), plus what has
been done to keep the dog healthy.

Explain the right way to obedience train a dog,
and demonstrate three comments.

Several of the requirements have to do with health
care, including first aid, handling a hurt dog, and
the dangers of home treatment for a serious
ailment.

The final requirement is to know the local laws
and ordinances involving dogs.

There are similar programs for Girl Scouts and 4-H
members.

Local Clubs

Local dog clubs are no longer in existence just to put
on a yearly dog show. Today, they are apt to be the hub
of the community's involvement with pets. Dog clubs
conduct educational forums with big-name speakers,
stage demonstrations of canine talent in a busy mall
and take dogs of various breeds to schools for classroom discussion.

The quickest way to feel accepted as a member in a
club is to volunteer your services! Offer to help with
something—anything—and watch your popularity
(and your interest) grow.

Therapy Dogs

Once your dog has earned that essential CGC and reliably demonstrates a steady, calm temperament, you could look into what therapy dogs are doing in your area.

Therapy dogs go with their owners to visit patients at hospitals or nursing homes, generally remaining on leash but able to coax a pat from a stiffened hand, a smile from a blank face, a few words from sealed lips or a hug from someone in need of love.

Nursing homes cover a wide range of patient care. Some specialize in care of the elderly, some in the treatment of specific illnesses, some in physical therapy. Children's facilities also welcome visits from trained therapy dogs for boosting morale in their pediatric patients. Hospice care for the terminally ill and the at-home care of AIDS patients are other areas where this canine visiting is desperately needed. Therapy dog training comes first.

Your dog can make a difference in lots of lives.

There is a lot more involved than just taking your nice friendly pooch to someone's bedside. Doing therapy dog work involves your own emotional stability as well as that of your dog. But once you have met all the requirements for this work, making the rounds once a week or once a month with your therapy dog is possibly the most rewarding of all community activities.

Disaster Aid

This community service is definitely not for everyone, partly because it is time-consuming. The initial training is rigorous, and there can be no let-up in the continuing workouts, because members are on call 24 hours a day to go wherever they are needed at a moment's notice. But if you think you would like to be able to assist in a disaster, look into search-and-rescue work. The network of search-and-rescue volunteers is worldwide, and all members of the American Rescue Dog Association (ARDA) who are qualified to do this work are volunteers who train and maintain their own dogs.

Physical Aid

Most people are familiar with Seeing Eye dogs, which serve as blind people's eyes, but not with all the other work that dogs are trained to do to assist the disabled. Dogs are also specially trained to pull wheelchairs, carry school books, pick up dropped objects, open and close doors. Some also are ears for the deaf. All these assistance-trained dogs, by the way, are allowed anywhere "No Pet" signs exist (as are therapy dogs when

Making the rounds with your therapy dog can be very rewarding.

properly identified). Getting started in any of this fascinating work requires a background in dog training and canine behavior, but there are also volunteer jobs ranging from answering the phone to cleaning out kennels to providing a foster home for a puppy. You have only to ask.

Beyond
the
Basics

Recommended Reading

Books

ABOUT HEALTH CARE

Ackerman, Lowell. *Guide to Skin and Haircoat Problems in Dogs.* Loveland, Colo.: Alpine Publications, 1994.

Alderton, David. *The Dog Care Manual.* Hauppauge, N.Y.: Barron's Educational Series, Inc., 1986.

American Kennel Club. *American Kennel Club Dog Care and Training.* New York: Howell Book House, 1991.

Bamberger, Michelle, DVM. *Help! The Quick Guide to First Aid for Your Dog.* New York: Howell Book House, 1995.

Carlson, Delbert, DVM, and James Giffin, MD. *Dog Owner's Home Veterinary Handbook.* New York: Howell Book House, 1992.

DeBitetto, James, DVM, and Sarah Hodgson. *You & Your Puppy.* New York: Howell Book House, 1995.

Humphries, Jim, DVM. *Dr. Jim's Animal Clinic for Dogs.* New York: Howell Book House, 1994.

McGinnis, Terri. *The Well Dog Book.* New York: Random House, 1991.

Pitcairn, Richard and Susan. *Natural Health for Dogs.* Emmaus, Pa.: Rodale Press, 1982.

ABOUT DOG SHOWS

Hall, Lynn. *Dog Showing for Beginners.* New York: Howell Book House, 1994.

Nichols, Virginia Tuck. *How to Show Your Own Dog.* Neptune, N. J.: TFH, 1970.

Vanacore, Connie. *Dog Showing, An Owner's Guide.* New York: Howell Book House, 1990.

ABOUT TRAINING

Ammen, Amy. *Training in No Time*. New York: Howell Book House, 1995.

Baer, Ted. *Communicating With Your Dog*. Hauppauge, N.Y.: Barron's Educational Series, Inc., 1989.

Benjamin, Carol Lea. *Dog Problems*. New York: Howell Book House, 1989.

Benjamin, Carol Lea. *Dog Training for Kids*. New York: Howell Book House, 1988.

Benjamin, Carol Lea. *Mother Knows Best*. New York: Howell Book House, 1985.

Benjamin, Carol Lea. *Surviving Your Dog's Adolescence*. New York: Howell Book House, 1993.

Bohnenkamp, Gwen. *Manners for the Modern Dog*. San Francisco: Perfect Paws, 1990.

Dibra, Bashkim. *Dog Training by Bash*. New York: Dell, 1992.

Dunbar, Ian, PhD, MRCVS. *Dr. Dunbar's Good Little Dog Book*, James & Kenneth Publishers, 2140 Shattuck Ave. #2406, Berkeley, Calif. 94704. (510) 658–8588. Order from the publisher.

Dunbar, Ian, PhD, MRCVS. *How to Teach a New Dog Old Tricks*, James & Kenneth Publishers. Order from the publisher; address above.

Dunbar, Ian, PhD, MRCVS, and Gwen Bohnenkamp. Booklets on *Preventing Aggression; Housetraining; Chewing; Digging; Barking; Socialization; Fearfulness; and Fighting*, James & Kenneth Publishers. Order from the publisher; address above.

Evans, Job Michael. *People, Pooches and Problems*. New York: Howell Book House, 1991.

Kilcommons, Brian and Sarah Wilson. *Good Owners, Great Dogs*. New York: Warner Books, 1992.

McMains, Joel M. *Dog Logic—Companion Obedience*. New York: Howell Book House, 1992.

Rutherford, Clarice and David H. Neil, MRCVS. *How to Raise a Puppy You Can Live With*. Loveland, Colo.: Alpine Publications, 1982.

Volhard, Jack and Melissa Bartlett. *What All Good Dogs Should Know: The Sensible Way to Train*. New York: Howell Book House, 1991.

ABOUT BREEDING

Harris, Beth J. Finder. *Breeding a Litter, The Complete Book of Prenatal and Postnatal Care*. New York: Howell Book House, 1983.

Holst, Phyllis, DVM. *Canine Reproduction*. Loveland, Colo.: Alpine Publications, 1985.

Walkowicz, Chris and Bonnie Wilcox, DVM. *Successful Dog Breeding, The Complete Handbook of Canine Midwifery.* New York: Howell Book House, 1994.

ABOUT ACTIVITIES

American Rescue Dog Association. *Search and Rescue Dogs.* New York: Howell Book House, 1991.

Barwig, Susan and Stewart Hilliard. *Schutzhund.* New York: Howell Book House, 1991.

Beaman, Arthur S. *Lure Coursing.* New York: Howell Book House, 1994.

Daniels, Julie. *Enjoying Dog Agility—From Backyard to Competition.* New York: Doral Publishing, 1990.

Davis, Kathy Diamond. *Therapy Dogs.* New York: Howell Book House, 1992.

Gallup, Davis Anne. *Running With Man's Best Friend.* Loveland, Colo.: Alpine Publications, 1986.

Habgood, Dawn and Robert. *On the Road Again With Man's Best Friend.* New England, Mid-Atlantic, West Coast and Southeast editions. Selective guides to area bed and breakfasts, inns, hotels and resorts that welcome guests and their dogs. New York: Howell Book House, 1995.

Holland, Vergil S. *Herding Dogs.* New York: Howell Book House, 1994.

LaBelle, Charlene G. *Backpacking With Your Dog.* Loveland, Colo.: Alpine Publications, 1993.

Simmons-Moake, Jane. *Agility Training, The Fun Sport for All Dogs.* New York: Howell Book House, 1991.

Spencer, James B. *Hup! Training Flushing Spaniels the American Way.* New York: Howell Book House, 1992.

Spencer, James B. *Point! Training the All-Seasons Birddog.* New York: Howell Book House, 1995.

Tarrant, Bill. *Training the Hunting Retriever.* New York: Howell Book House, 1991.

Volhard, Jack and Wendy. *The Canine Good Citizen.* New York: Howell Book House, 1994.

General Titles

Haggerty, Captain Arthur J. *How to Get Your Pet Into Show Business.* New York: Howell Book House, 1994.

McLennan, Bardi. *Dogs and Kids, Parenting Tips.* New York: Howell Book House, 1993.

Moran, Patti J. *Pet Sitting for Profit, A Complete Manual for Professional Success.* New York: Howell Book House, 1992.

Scalisi, Danny and Libby Moses. *When Rover Just Won't Do, Over 2,000 Suggestions for Naming Your Dog.* New York: Howell Book House, 1993.

Sife, Wallace, PhD. *The Loss of a Pet.* New York: Howell Book House, 1993.

Wrede, Barbara J. *Civilizing Your Puppy.* Hauppauge, N.Y.: Barron's Educational Series, 1992.

Magazines

The AKC GAZETTE, The Official Journal for the Sport of Purebred Dogs. American Kennel Club, 51 Madison Ave., New York, NY.

Bloodlines Journal. United Kennel Club, 100 E. Kilgore Rd., Kalamazoo, MI.

Dog Fancy. Fancy Publications, 3 Burroughs, Irvine, CA 92718

Dog World. Maclean Hunter Publishing Corp., 29 N. Wacker Dr., Chicago, IL 60606.

Videos

"SIRIUS Puppy Training," by Ian Dunbar, PhD, MRCVS. James & Kenneth Publishers, 2140 Shattuck Ave. #2406, Berkeley, CA 94704. Order from the publisher.

"Training the Companion Dog," from Dr. Dunbar's British TV Series, James & Kenneth Publishers. (See address above).

The American Kennel Club produces videos on every breed of dog, as well as on hunting tests, field trials and other areas of interest to purebred dog owners. For more information, write to AKC/Video Fulfillment, 5580 Centerview Dr., Suite 200, Raleigh, NC 27606.

chapter 13

Resources

Breed Clubs

Every breed recognized by the American Kennel Club has a national (parent) club. National clubs are a great source of information on your breed. You can get the name of the secretary of the club by contacting:

The American Kennel Club
51 Madison Avenue
New York, NY 10010
(212) 696-8200

There are also numerous all-breed, individual breed, obedience, hunting and other special-interest dog clubs across the country. The American Kennel Club can provide you with a geographical list of clubs to find ones in your area. Contact them at the above address.

Registry Organizations

Registry organizations register purebred dogs. The American Kennel Club is the oldest and largest in this country, and currently recognizes over 130 breeds. The United Kennel Club registers some breeds the AKC doesn't (including the American Pit Bull Terrier and the Miniature Fox Terrier) as well as many of the same breeds. The others included here are for your reference; the AKC can provide you with a list of foreign registries.

American Kennel Club
51 Madison Avenue
New York, NY 10010

United Kennel Club (UKC)
100 E. Kilgore Road
Kalamazoo, MI 49001-5598

American Dog Breeders Assn.
P.O. Box 1771
Salt Lake City, UT 84110
(Registers American Pit Bull Terriers)

Canadian Kennel Club
89 Skyway Avenue
Etobicoke, Ontario
Canada M9W 6R4

National Stock Dog Registry
P.O. Box 402
Butler, IN 46721
(Registers working stock dogs)

Orthopedic Foundation for Animals (OFA)
2300 E. Nifong Blvd.
Columbia, MO 65201-3856
(Hip registry)

Activity Clubs

Write to these organizations for information on the
activities they sponsor.

American Kennel Club
51 Madison Avenue
New York, NY 10010
(Conformation Shows, Obedience Trials, Field
Trials and Hunting Tests, Agility, Canine Good

Citizen, Lure Coursing, Herding, Tracking,
Earthdog Tests, Coonhunting.)

United Kennel Club
100 E. Kilgore Road
Kalamazoo, MI 49001-5598
(Conformation Shows, Obedience Trials, Agility,
Hunting for Various Breeds, Terrier Trials and
more.)

North American Flyball Assn.
1342 Jeff St.
Ypsilanti, MI 48198

International Sled Dog Racing Assn.
P.O. Box 446
Norman, ID 83848-0446

North American Working Dog Assn., Inc.
Southeast Kreisgruppe
P.O. Box 833
Brunswick, GA 31521

Trainers

Association of Pet Dog Trainers
P.O. Box 385
Davis, CA 95617
(800) PET–DOGS

American Dog Trainers' Network
161 West 4th St.
New York, NY 10014
(212) 727–7257

**National Association of Dog Obedience
Instructors**
2286 East Steel Rd.
St. Johns, MI 48879

Beyond the
Basics

Associations

American Dog Owners Assn.
1654 Columbia Tpk.
Castleton, NY 12033
(Combats anti-dog legislation)

Delta Society
P.O. Box 1080
Renton, WA 98057-1080
(Promotes the human/animal bond through
pet-assisted therapy and other programs)

Dog Writers Assn. of America (DWAA)
Sally Cooper, Secy.
222 Woodchuck Ln.
Harwinton, CT 06791

National Assn. for Search and Rescue (NASAR)
P.O. Box 3709
Fairfax, VA 22038

Therapy Dogs International
6 Hilltop Road
Mendham, NJ 07945